Walking in the Chilterns

ELIZABETH CULL

ROBERT HALE · LONDON

ISBN 0 7090 4145 4

Robert Hale Limited
Clerkenwell House
Clerkenwell Green
London EC1R 0HT

Map artwork by Ken Johnston

Photoset in North Wales by
Derek Doyle & Associates, Mold, Clwyd.
Printed in Great Britain by
St Edmundsbury Press, Bury St Edmunds, Suffolk.
Bound by Woolnough Limited.

Elizabeth Cull was born and brought up in London, and was very happy to move to the Chilterns in 1958 to be closer to the countryside. She became familiar with the hills and byways on evening walks and weekend rambles, and when the Ridgeway LDFP was created in 1973 she wrote her first book – *Walks Along the* ... was followed by *Walks in the Lake* *of the Chilterns* and (with Elizabeth ...*re of Buckinghamshire*. While *Walking in* ...*erns* was in preparation, the author moved to ...ng and now lives below the hills, near to the Grand Union Canal and within sight of the Bridgewater Monument at Ashridge.

Contents

Introduction

In spring, when beech leaves are softening the woods with a green haze, or on blustery days in autumn when we wake to clouds driven before the wind in massed purple and gold and our feet itch for distant, inaccessible rocks and heather, the low green hills of the Chilterns wait for us not an hour away from Marylebone.

I wouldn't pretend that this easy, intimate country is any rival to Yorkshire, Teesdale or the Lake District, but for those of us who live in the soft south, the area does offer days and weekends of fine walking throughout the year when all else is far away. Apart from the long-distance walks, a maze of footpaths kept in order by local authorities and by widely supported amenity societies, such as the Chiltern Society, leads from village to lovely village, across fields and through ancient beech woods, beside rivers and canals and up and down over hills and chalk grasslands that can be walked without difficulty by young and old alike.

What better use could one make of a long summer day than to take an early train from Marylebone to Princes Risborough and follow the Ridgeway north-east over Whiteleaf Hill and Pulpit Hill towards Wendover, to picnic on Coombe Hill or lunch at one of the four or five ancient inns or two teashops in Wendover's broad High Street; then, refreshed, to climb again through Hale Wood and over Hastoe Hill and come down towards evening to Tring Park, sauntering there with shadows long on the ground, making for Tring station and a train back to Euston? Fifteen magical miles, by any standard.

That is but one walk among many; its counterpart in pleasure can be found over and over along the lines of footpaths, byways and bridlepaths on OS map 165, 175, 174 and 166 which cover the area. The difficulty for those not familiar with the Chilterns is knowing where to start and which of the many paths to follow – a difficulty which I hope this book will resolve.

Before we go any further, it might be wise to define the area. This is never easy, since 'the Chilterns' is one of those vague descriptions like 'Snowdonia' or 'the Yorkshire Dales' – areas with no fixed boundaries, so that everyone knows where they are, roughly, and knows when they are in the Chilterns or Snowdonia or the Dales, but just when they set foot over the border is never easy to tell. I have suggested the OS maps above as covering the Chilterns, but by no stretch of the imagination could the whole of the area shown on those maps be called 'Chilterns'. Nor can we define the area as that covered by the Chiltern Hundreds, which were three groups of parishes in South Buckinghamshire formerly the Hundreds, or administrative units, of Desborough, Burnham and Stoke. Stoke, with the parishes of Eton, Slough, Datchet and Colnbrook, among others, is really Thames Valley. Burnham also had a large chunk of Slough; Desborough, which runs west from High Wycombe, does better, but still takes in only a tiny part of the Chilterns. I prefer to take for reference that area covered by No. 159 in the old OS 1-inch series, which bore the title 'Chilterns' and which covered the whole run of the hills, leaving out Slough, Reading and Windsor in the south-eastern corner.

The Chiltern Hills stretch for 45 miles to the north-west of London, from Dunstable to the Thames, never rising much above 800 feet, and marking the outer edge of that tilted plate of chalk that underlies the clay of the London basin. The chalk face drops away sharply on its north face, giving spectacular views to the walker on the hilltops across the Vale of Aylesbury and the Oxfordshire plain. On the gentler southern slopes a richness of common flowers awaits those with eyes to see: bluebells, anenomes, primroses, violets, ramsons, wood sorrel and herb Robert in the beech woods, cowslips on the chalk grasslands and coltsfoot on the rough margins, and hedgerows alive through spring and summer with blackthorn, hawthorn, dog rose, guelder rose and honeysuckle, bringing on the bright berries of autumn – a joyous place indeed for a walker.

A book such as this cannot hope to cover every lovely walk or every footpath in a place that so abounds in them. I have tried to use those which are most accessible and those which give the best introduction to the district. As you tackle the long-distance routes or try those shorter walks described in detail, other walks will readily suggest themselves. A glance along a lane in passing or an attractive footpath crossing the way will lead you to study the maps and work out routes of your own. These are often the best walks – the carefree setting forth without the discipline of a set of instructions to follow, only the path to wander or the heath to cross. Suggestions for further exploration are offered in the chapters of short walks; and remember, it is impossible to find yourself benighted in the Chilterns!

Overall the Chilterns is not a large area, and walks are bound to overlap and, in some instances, use the same paths; in such cases it has been necessary to repeat instructions. Walks centred on Tring, Wendover and Chesham all tend to overlap around Cholesbury and Hastoe, just as those centred on Wendover, Great Missenden and Amersham overlap around the Hampdens. In truth, this becomes an advantage in time as, with greater knowledge of the district, the overlapping paths become old friends, so that you will find yourself leaving this book more and more on the shelf as you work out your own best-loved walks. I have preferred to repeat instructions in the few places necessary rather than to attempt the cumbersome, and often confusing, use of devices such as 'turn to page (say) 42 and follow the instructions until the old mill by the stream is reached'.

One problem faces us in this inhabited area which doesn't so often arise on the northern pathways: footpaths get diverted and routes closed off, temporarily or permanently, by development – as I discovered in the course of writing this book, when I had to wait two years for the completion of the Amersham bypass to be sure where the footpaths would go. Also, explicit directions to 'bear left past the white-painted gate' or 'follow the fence as far as the bridge' are invalidated when the gate falls down or the fence is removed to make way for the building of someone's dream cottage. Instructions for the short walks and their associated sketch maps should always be used in conjunction with the appropriate OS map.

In any case, a wise walker should never rely on sketch maps alone. Not only are they useless if you stray from the prescribed route, but they leave you without ready means of escape should any member of the party injure themselves or become overtired. In such an event you could be no more than half a mile from a railway station or bus stop or have a quick escape route back to your car, and not know it. But while the OS map shows every facet of the terrain it does not indicate, as this book will try to do, the best and prettiest paths.

Maps used are the OS 1/50,000 Landranger series, and in some instances a grid reference is given. Those of you who know about grid references should skip the next paragraph, but if you've previously dodged round the subject please read on. Interpreting the numbers is necessary, and very simple, once you get the hang of it.

The grid reference, or GR, is based on the square grid lines marked on OS maps and the associated numbers printed along the top and bottom and down both sides of the sheet. On the Landranger series these numbers are conveniently repeated across the face of the map, down and across, at every twentieth square. The numbers from left to right are known as Eastings because they increase to the east, and the numbers from bottom to top are known as Northings, because they increase to the north. In the six-figure GR the first and second figures refer to the numbers across the sheet – the Eastings, and the fourth and fifth figures refer to the numbers up the sheet – the Northings. As an example, the village of Wingrave on OS 165 lies at the intersection of Easting line 87 with Northing line 19, giving a GR of 870190. Similarly, Rowsham, nearby, lies at the intersection of Easting 85 with Northing 18, to become GR 850180. Now we come to the complicated bit. Where we are not so fortunate as to have our reference at the intersection of two lines, but find it stuck out in the middle of the square, as at Rowsham Bridge, we have to estimate the position in relation to the nearest Easting to the left of it and the nearest Northing below it, on a scale of tenths. So Rowsham Bridge, being just over halfway between Easting lines 84 and 85, would have an Easting of 84 and six tenths, written as 846; and being in the same relation to Northing lines 17 and 18, the village would have a Northing of 17 and six tenths, written as 176, giving a six figure reference for Rowsham Bridge of GR 846176. Practise this with a few places taken at random and you'll soon get used to it; but if you should forget, you can always turn back to this paragraph and work it out again.

I am often asked the significance of the numbers which sometimes appear on official footpath (FP) signs. These are the numbers assigned to the paths on the County definitive maps, which can be seen at local council offices. The numbers are not shown on OS maps, nor are they shown as a matter of course on all FP signs, so although I know they are used in some books of walks, I prefer to ignore them. It seems pointless to go to all the trouble of working out path numbers when their use on footpath signs is by no means universal.

However, you won't have to bother with GRs or FP numbers for the long-distance routes, as they are obligingly waymarked for us. There are three of these waymarked routes in the Chilterns of which the first, the Ridgeway LDFP which follows the hills from Ivinghoe to Goring, is probably the best known and most used. The second is the North Bucks Way, a 30 mile chain of footpaths starting at Chequers Knap above Kimble and ending within sight of the new city of Milton Keynes. The third is the Oxfordshire Way, from the Cotswolds to the Chilterns, starting on the banks of the Windrush at Bourton on the Water and ending at Henley. The last two routes were pioneered by branches of the Ramblers' Association, and the North Bucks Way continues to be waymarked by them. The idea for the Oxfordshire Way came from members of the Oxfordshire Field Paths Society, and they share the credit for tramping out that route and waymarking it.

A great deal is owed to the Ramblers' Association by anyone who enjoys a walk in the country. The Association is active in the protection of the countryside in general, and of footpaths and rights of way in particular; and our present freedom to walk in the woods and on the moors and mountains is almost entirely due to the agitation of RA members and sympathizers during the 1920s and 30s, when the scenes at the moor edges in Derbyshire or Lancashire (after the word had gone round that a mass trespass was to be attempted) resembled what we saw on our television sets in the 1980s during the miners' strike, with gamekeepers taking on the role of police.

It is hard to credit that as little as fifty years ago the open moors and woodlands we take for granted were in many cases forbidden territory to the ordinary walker. Customary footpaths and rights of way linked the villages, but little else was available. The launching of the Ramblers' Association as a national body in 1935 was a very positive step in the opening up of the countryside, and you could say that all our present long-distance routes stem from the proposal by the legendary Tom Stephenson, RA's first full-time secretary, for a 'long green trail' along the spine of England. The resulting Pennine Way Association kept pushing the idea of this and other long-distance footpaths throughout the war years, and their pressure led, via the National Parks and Access to the Countryside Act of 1949, to the opening of the Pennine Way as the first LDFP on 24th April 1965. This was followed by the Cleveland Way in May 1969, the Pembrokeshire Coast Path in May 1970 and Offa's Dyke Path in July 1971. Our own Ridgeway LDFP, opened in September 1973, was a comparative Johnny-come-lately.

Unlike the northern long-distance routes, you can walk the Chiltern footpaths and LDFPs at any time of year. You don't find snow poles beside Chiltern roads, and though we get our share of winter weather and the going might sometimes be unpleasantly muddy and slippery underfoot, anyone who has slogged through peat hags on Kinder, dragged through heather on the North York Moors or struggled against wind and snow on Cross Fell will find the Chiltern routes always easy walking.

While on the subject of Long-Distance Footpaths, I'd like to explode the myth, most often mentioned in connection with the Pennine Way, about the route being marked from end to end with orange peel, drink cans and general litter. I have never found this so. In my experience most walkers are tidy souls, more inclined to gather up litter for disposal than to strew it around.

For those who like, or need, level terrain, the waterside routes are recommended, particularly the main towpath to the Grand Union Canal or the Wendover and Aylesbury arms. Here are true quietness and solitude; there is hardly a house, for instance, along the whole 7 miles of· the Aylesbury arm, but there are reed buntings and butterflies along the banks, solitary heron and flocks of lapwings rising from the fields nearby, and the continual song of skylarks. The Thames route is different again, busy with boats and people almost all the way, but another level walk and an interesting and not particularly taxing one.

The grouped walks are all centred on railway stations. The Chiltern area is well served with trains: from Marylebone to Wendover, Aylesbury and Princes Risborough; from Baker Street to Rickmansworth, Amersham and Chesham and from Euston to Berkhamsted and Tring. Most of the stations are supplied with carparks which are empty and free at weekends. However, suggestions are also given for suitable carparks along the routes.

There are notes on birds, flowers and butterflies, confined to the author's limited knowledge or means of enquiry, and on items of interest along the way. Walkers interested in flora and fauna (and few are not) are recommended to the BBONT nature reserve handbook entitled *Where to Go For Wildlife in Bucks, Berks & Oxfordshire*, published by the Berks, Bucks & Oxfordshire Naturalists' Trust (see bibliography). With the help of this book and a measure of assiduity a great deal can be seen that might otherwise be missed. As an instance, their Chequers Reserve, which they manage by agreement with the Chequers Estate and which lies beside the route of the Ridgeway LDFP, is reported in the handbook as having 'interesting chalk grassland plants including rock rose, thyme, squinancywort, vipers bugloss, deadly nightshade and the Musk orchid', and it is also reported that the box coombs there, themselves world famous, contain one of the richest assemblages of chalk-loving mosses and liverworts in the Chilterns. This is one of the reserves open to permit holders only (moral: become a member and receive notice of conducted tours). BBONT also publishes a very readable and informative book on flora and fauna entitled *Wild Life of the Thames Counties*, with some pretty spectacular pictures, including several of wild orchids and one of a stoat standing over a just-killed rabbit.

Finally, on your walks give a thought to those who care for the Chilterns: the National Trust, those good landlords whose NT mark is found all over the maps of the area; the Chiltern Society, whose members clear footpaths, mend stiles, and keep a general watching brief; BBONT; the Herts & Middx Naturalists' Trust; the Ramblers' Association and Oxfordshire Field Paths Society aforementioned; Young Farmers Clubs, who clear copses and trim and lay hedges; the Youth Hostels Association, whose members cleared the scrub on Pitstone Hill, and the countless smaller organizations and individuals who waymark, clear paths, dredge ponds and generally keep the place alive.

Abbreviations

CP	Car park
P	Parking
GR	Grid reference
BR	British Rail
FP	Footpath

LDFP	Long-distance footpath
OS	Ordnance Survey
RA	Ramblers' Association
NBW	North Bucks Way
BBONT	Berks, Bucks and Oxfordshire Naturalists' Trust
SSSI	Sites of Special Scientific Interest
CPRE	Council for the Preservation of Rural England

1 Walks in the Hills from Tring

There are many fine walks in the Chilterns, taken as a whole, but what distinguishes the district from other walking country in the south-east is the range of hills that gives it a name. They are not the highest of hills – rising nowhere to much above 800 feet, so never difficult of ascent – yet they are high enough to give exhilarating, windblown ridge walks and high enough, too, to show rewarding vistas from their summits across what Rupert Brooke described as 'the sleeping Midland plain' ('Chilterns', 1913).

The hills lie in a diagonal band from Whipsnade in the north-east, where the Dunstable Downs slope into Bedfordshire, to Watlington in the south-west, where the Chiltern Hills descend to the Thames Valley. Once the whole range could be found on the OS inch to the mile 159, but now we need the metricated 165 and 175 to cover the same area. I understand the Survey has now decided against printing their projected *Chilterns* map in the Outdoor Leisure series on the grounds that there is 'no demand'. Perhaps we should all write and tell them otherwise.

Since it would be unwieldy, to say the least, to try to cover all the hills in one chapter, I have sectioned them off into three parts, roughly comprising Ivinghoe to Tring (this chapter), Wendover to Whiteleaf (Chapter 2) and Chinnor to Watlington (Chapter 3). Some valley walks are included in these sections where they do not fit neatly into any other chapter.

The length of the Chilterns ridge is now dominated by the Ridgeway LDFP, specifically dealt with in Chapter 6. You will find this path mentioned throughout, not only as a useful marker but, inevitably, because it follows the ancient Icknield Way along the most obvious ridge route. Sections of the Icknield Way are now best avoided by walkers since these sections are used today, apparently as of right, by rough country trail raiders on motorbikes and four-wheel drive cars. It wouldn't be so bad if these Green-roaders, as they call themselves, stuck to the drove road over which they claim a right of way; unfortunately they stray over the surrounding land so that the whole area becomes a morass. Here they are worse than the horse riders, who cause us trouble enough by not sticking to their bridle paths, since, on the whole, horse riders tend to go out for an hour or two only which largely restricts them to an area, but nowhere is out of reach of the trail riders, as I discovered in Ennerdale the other year.

I was once informed that the only persons with true right to take wheeled vehicles over drove roads were those who owned or farmed the land abutting. I am not qualified to argue the case, and can only advise walkers of the worst stretches so that they might avoid them.

We start, then, at the top of the map with the north-western sections from Ivinghoe to the Tring gap, an area most conveniently reached from Tring or Berkhamsted stations on the London Euston to Birmingham New Street line. Weekday parking for drivers is not a problem as there are numerous laybys and roadside areas that are used as mini parking spots, though I am against leaving cars dotted all over the countryside and always try to use a proper carpark, even if it adds a mile or so to my walk. At weekends there is ample free parking at Tring station (which, it should be noted, is a good mile from Tring town, so don't try parking there). There is no station carpark at Berkhamsted, as such, but ample parking is in the town a few steps away.

It will soon become obvious as you follow these walks that the area is criss-crossed with footpaths giving, in combination, countless satisfying and beautiful walks, of which only a few can be described here. Dacorum Borough Council issues an excellent booklet (see bibliography) describing thirty-three walks in the area bounded by the M1 motorway, the Chiltern Hills and the A41, with excursions south-east to Flaunden and Chipperfield – a great many walks for a comparatively small area.

Walk 1

Tring station – Pitstone Hill via Ridgeway LDFP – Ivinghoe Beacon – Clipper Down – Bridgewater Monument – Aldbury

(10 miles)

ALTERNATIVE
Start and finish at Aldbury
(8 miles)

OS map 165
Sketch map 1

P Tring station carpark GR 952123
Aldbury village GR 966124
Station: Tring BR

The first walk in this section is one without which any book on walking in the Chilterns would be incomplete: the classic route from Tring over Pitstone Hill to Ivinghoe Beacon, returning via the Ivinghoe Hills, Clipper Down, Moneybury Hill, Ashridge and Aldbury. Aldbury is the archetypal English village: perpendicular church, pond, stocks, village shops and inns, old smithy and bakehouse, thatched timber-framed and white-daubed cottages, all lying below the ridge of brooding, wooded hills. The village has the luck to lie at the junction of several minor roads leading to nowhere in particular, and in consequence is silent and peaceful throughout the week, though it does get busier at weekends.

Twenty years ago this was the finest walk in the Chilterns, through woods and over chalk grasslands with extensive views to the west and north over the Vale of Aylesbury and north-east to Whipsnade and Dunstable Downs. Then the ribs of chalk were covered with springy turf; now time and a million pairs of boots have eroded the turf from the hilltops, and affluence in the form of the horse and the motorcyle has muddied the valley bottoms. But the views are there still, as are the shy spring flowers, the dog roses

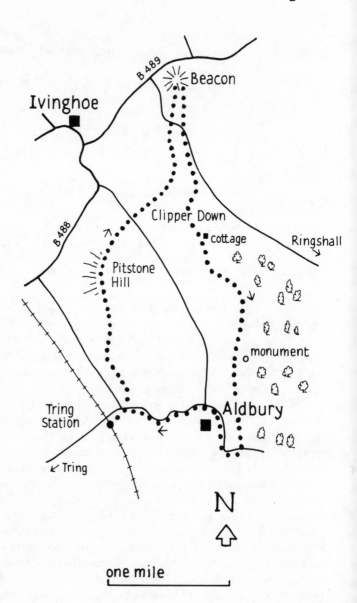

Map 1

B 489

Beacon

Ivinghoe

Clipper Down

cottage

Ringshall

B 488

Pitstone
Hill

monument

Tring
Station

Aldbury

← Tring

N

one mile

of summer, and the glorious autumn beeches dressed in every glowing shade from russet to amber. And the wind still blows clean and fresh along the ridge. Wear good boots or wellingtons with a deep tread, pick up a stick to help on the slippery bits, and you will still have an exhilarating and enjoyable walk.

From Tring station turn right along the road for a short distance to pass the Pitstone road junction. Just past this junction a Ridgeway LDFP sign poins you up a bridlepath towards a house on the left; take this, and keep straight on beside the hedge when the paved drive goes off left and you will come to the LDFP ahead; turn left onto the path for a fine 2-mile walk. The route first winds uphill through woods, then follows the contour of Pitstone Hill with the ridge rising on the right. Violets and primroses line the path here in spring and early summer, and later, in good years, the chalk grassland is scattered with cowslips. As you leave Pitstone behind in the valley below, the path descends to cross a narrow road beside a grassy carpark and enters the field opposite, where sheep graze. Soon the way climbs again to a stile and rises uphill to another stile and wide gate.

From this point the LDFP descends to cross a narrow lane before rising to Ivinghoe Beacon. This stretch of the path is broad, slippery and lethal. Every vestige of grass and topsoil has been gouged away, exposing the bare chalk. Not only is it dangerous, it is positively cruel to the ground to walk upon it. Turn aside instead and, without climbing the stile, take the narrow footpath on the left which will take you in roughly the same direction, also to cross the lane before rising to the Beacon.

I confess to finding the summit of Ivinghoe Beacon something of a let-down. The very word 'Beacon', coupled with the view from below of a massive, brooding eminence, raises expectations. One gazes up and wonders what will mark the summit. A Lakeland-type cairn, perhaps; or a pile of faggots ready for the torch? Or even, the hope rises in bad weather, some sort of windbreak like the Celtic wall above Ribblesdale or the great shelter cross on Helvellyn? But no, there is not so much as a rock to put your back against – just an OS trig point on a broad, grassy summit – though there are wonderful views in all directions, a good enough aim for any walk.

The return journey follows the Ridgeway back down from the Beacon across the unfenced road to Ringshall crossed on the way up, but once across that road it strikes, almost immediately, another clear path to the left of the LDFP. This path rises to keep company with the road, though well above it, until it clears the trees. Keep left when the path divides and you will emerge onto a stretch of high, windblown heath. Dunstable Downs stretch away to the left, with the white lion of Whipsnade carved into the chalk above them.

There is a proliferation of paths here, but keep to the left and you will stay with the good view, coming down eventually beside the road to a green stretch used, regrettably, as a carpark. (A better carpark is behind you on the other side of the road.) Cross this short green stretch to the far end where a footpath goes off right, alongside the private road to Clipper Down Cottage. This footpath descends eventually to a dip where it is blocked by a fence ahead. Turn right here onto the bridlepath and follow it to Clipper Down Cottage, where dogs will bark, passing through the gate to the right and continuing ahead. Again, you may be confused on this stretch by crossing paths, but keep broadly south and you will strike the bridlepath.

Soon the route becomes a broad, southerly ride descending gradually through the trees, with occasional fine glimpses on your right to the valley below. Some 3 miles from the Beacon you will come upon a ruined cottage in a clearing beside a National Trust notice. From here there are many paths, very muddy in places and with ways crossing and converging on the Ridgeway LDFP, but if you remember that your route is southerly you will come out at or near the Bridgewater Monument, standing in a clearing beside a walkers' shelter and a National Trust shop and tea place.

The return to Aldbury village is simple. Take the broad path that passes in front of the shop and Monument Cottage, bearing SSW. Keep right on an obvious descending southerly path and you will emerge after a scant mile in Aldbury, where the Trooper on your left or the Greyhound on your right serve refreshments, and the farmhouse opposite the Greyhound serves cream teas.

Tring station is the best part of another mile away along the road past the church, in Station Road.

Car drivers wishing to start and finish at Aldbury will find a small carpark beside the pond where the village green once was. To join the walk, pass the church along Station Road (or walk through the churchyard, where there are interesting old gravestones and markers outside, and inside a magnificent perpendicular screen, encaustic tiles and fifteenth-century effigies; in 1988 there were sheep grazing in the churchyard: black sheep!). 50 yards along Station Road at Church Farm the FP sign points you across the farm lands to 'Pitstone Hill, 1½', but well before this 1½ miles are up you will join the LDFP in the woods crowning the rise ahead.

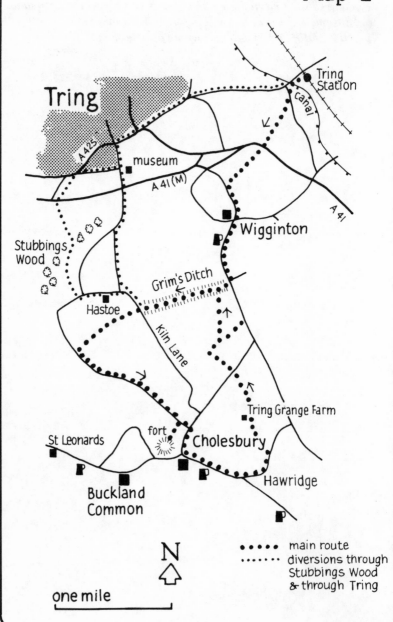

Map 2

Tring

Tring
Station

Canal

A425

museum

A 41(M)

A 41

Wigginton

P

Stubbings
Wood

Grim's Ditch

Hastoe

Kiln Lane

Tring Grange Farm

St Leonards

fort

Cholesbury

P

P

Hawridge

Buckland
Common

P

N

one mile

••••• main route
••••••• diversions through
Stubbings Wood
& through Tring

Walk 2

**Tring station – Wigginton – Grim's Ditch – Cholesbury –
Hawridge – Wigginton – Tring**

(10 miles)

ALTERNATIVES
Return from Grim's Ditch via Hastoe and Stubbings Wood
(8 miles)
Start and finish at Wigginton
(6 miles)

OS map 165
Sketch map 2

P Tring station carpark GR 952123
Greyhound Inn, Wigginton GR 939099 (for customers)
Station: Tring BR

The second walk from Tring station leaves the hills to go pleasantly by woods and farming country, visiting three or perhaps five villages which vary greatly in character: from workaday Wigginton, sprawling from its centre, to remote, tidy Hastoe and to ancient and well-preserved Cholesbury, Hawridge and St Leonards, skirting their high common below the wooded ridge.

If this were all the interest the walk offered it would be more than enough, but we also have 2 miles of Saxon earthworks and a vast Bronze Age fort, and you don't meet those attractions every day of the week.

The Saxon earthworks is marked on the OS map as Grim's Ditch, a name used commonly in the past to describe any phenomenon suspected of being unnatural, as anyone interested in small-scale maps will testify. The remains of this particular ditch can be traced in many places in the Chilterns. The original purpose is not known, but it has been dated at around AD 800 and is thought to have been a defensive boundary between Mercia and Wessex. Offa, King of Mercia, who 'Contended successfully against Wessex and the Welsh and made Mercia the principal state in England' (*Chambers Biographical Dictionary*) died in 796, and was the architect of that other great defensive boundary, Offa's Dyke. Like Offa's Dyke, our Grim's Ditch is a simple ditch and bank, still 10 foot deep in places, and here running almost unbroken from Wigginton to Buckland Wood, a little north of St Leonards.

The Bronze Age camp, or 'fort', is at Cholesbury, a great ditch and vallum, enclosing acres of land. The Saxons subsequently built their church within this well-defended site. David and Joan Hay's book *Hilltop Villages of the Chilterns* (see bibliography), available at any good bookshop or locally in the pubs, gives the history of the surrounding villages in detail: something for the long winter evenings, perhaps?

It is convenient to follow the Ridgeway LDFP from Tring station south-west towards Wigginton, so turn left from the station past the hotel, and left again at the first road junction. The LDFP will soon be found going SSW across fields on the right, eventually to cross the A41 and emerge at the outskirts of Wigginton in a road called The Twist. Turn left along this lane, passing Park Farm, and go straight on at the crossroads to take the Chesham road through the village until the last of the houses is left behind. Here, half a mile beyond the Greyhound, you will see a FP pointing right across fields. Take this westerly path to the far stile, where a green path slightly to the right keeps in the same direction. Soon Grim's Ditch will be on your left. Centuries of leaf-fall have rendered it almost level in places, and in places the rampart has gone, though the ditch remains; but the earthworks have been preserved in a lightly wooded strip between ploughed fields giving a heavenly walk through the beech leaves, with open fields to either side. To the left the view through the trees is of gentle, wooded slopes, and across the flat fields to the right are the trim buildings of Wick Farm that stand beside the Ridgeway Path.

After a mile the way wanders through a small copse to come to Kiln Road at a stile. Here the main route crosses to continue in the wood opposite at the marked FPs, but a diversion is possible. *Round the bend to the right to the tiny, tidy village of Hastoe which is worth a quick look. There is not so much as a pub, but some interesting houses, geese in a far garden and eggs for sale. As you enter the village a narrow paved lane goes due north to Tring, a steep hollow way going gloriously down between beech woods to come into Tring at Akeman Street alongside the Museum. Founded before the turn of the century by the second Lord Rothschild and left by him to the nation, Tring Museum is world famous for its collections, particularly of bird skins. On view to the public are beautifully preserved specimens of animals, birds, fish, butterflies and insects collected in the years when our consciences were less tender, so housed that one can go round the whole museum in an hour, though the temptation is to stay for days. If the weather deteriorates on the day of your walk, you could well consider turning back at Hastoe and walking the mile and a half into Tring.*

Another route to Tring from Hastoe is via Stubbings Wood. For this, continue through Hastoe village to the second turning on the right, signposted Hastoe Hill. Fifty yards past this turning a FP goes off right to take a north then north-east route to the bottom of the wood, when a right-hand turn will bring you to the museum. To return to the station after your visit, continue up Akeman Street to Tring High Street, where you turn right. Station Road will be found where the High Street ends, opposite the Robin Hood pub.

Back now to our main route, where we left it, crossing Kiln Road to re-enter the woods. Take the right-hand of the two footpaths offered, which continues beside the ditch to cross a bridlepath and come, within three-quarters of a mile, to a metalled lane. This is Shire Lane, the ancient boundary between Herts and Bucks. The OS map shows the route of Grim's Ditch continuing opposite, but between here and Hale Wood the earthworks is lost, and it is better to turn left along Shire Lane, when a pleasant tramp between beech woods will bring you, in a little under 2 miles, to Cholesbury. Cholesbury fort lies to the west of Shire Lane as it comes up to Cholesbury Common.

A narrow FP on the right as the Common comes in sight, just past a small post-enclosed carpark, will bring you to the earthworks in about 200 yards. The comparison with Grim's Ditch is immediate: the same great ditch with the earth flung up to form a rampart, but the ditch here is deeper, the bank higher, and the whole thing more impressive. This ditch encloses some 15 acres of land, and Cholesbury's originally Saxon church of St Lawrence was built within its confines. It is possible to walk around the ditch, either on the bank or along the bottom, leaving it over stiles at the causeway by the church when you will find yourself in the middle

of Cholesbury village. If you skip the fort and turn right at the top
of Shire Lane you will achieve the same result.

The walk continues eastwards around Cholesbury Common,
passing the cricket pitch, towards Hawridge and the Full Moon, a
pretty country pub with a great, sweet-smelling cream rose
spreading over the front wall and a windmill rising behind it. Being
run by pleasant people and having a nice garden, the Full Moon
gets very busy at weekends. (*Alternatives can be found in the Horse
& Hounds at Buckland Common or the White Lion at St Leonards,
either of which can be visited by turning left along the road at
Cholesbury for 800 yards to the Horse & Hounds and almost as far
again to the White Lion. If you are not pushed for time you will find
the diversion worthwhile for a snatch of rural England at its quiet
best.*)

To return to Wigginton, continue east round the Common past
the Full Moon until you join a paved road coming in from the left;
500 yards downhill here brings you to the farm road and bridleway
to Tring Farm on the left, a metalled byway which passes Tring
Farm to emerge onto Shire Lane in well under a mile. The route
then enters a wood opposite and goes due north through woodland
and meadow and plough to end in Wigginton beside the Grim's
Ditch stile, where an easy downhill walk through the village and
back to Tring station along the LDFP completes the day.

The OS map shows a FP from the centre of Wigginton village to
the A41 at New Ground, which might appear a reasonable route
back to the station, but in fact for most of the way it follows a
much-used bridlepath or heavy plough and is not recommended.

Walk 3

Berkhamsted station – Berkhamsted Castle – Frithsden Beeches – Northchurch Common – Berkhamsted

(5½ miles)

ALTERNATIVE
Visit Bridgewater Monument
(7½ miles)

OS map 165
Sketch map 3

P Berkhamsted station, or in the town GR 993082
Station: Berkhamsted BR

This next walk, above Berkhamsted, is a lovely late season walk, with brown crunchy leaves underfoot and frost riming the fields, and the bracken and beautiful beeches at Frithsden dressed in all the soft colours of autumn. It also gives an opportunity for a look at the Bridgewater Monument at Ashridge and a quick glance at Berkhamsted Castle. An ancient monument now in the care of the Ministry of Works, this is the remains of a castle built for Thomas à Becket on the site of a former edifice put up after 1066 by the Conqueror's half brother, Robert of Mortain. Entrance is 10p or a similar small amount, but you can see all you need to from the road.

From Berkhamsted station pass under the bridge and, with the castle on your right, continue up the road ahead to the signposted FP through the iron gate by the cricket club at the top. This path, nicely stiled, goes north for a mile across broad farmlands towards the woods crowning the rise ahead.

Take the left-hand path on entering the wood. After going sharply uphill for a short distance this emerges into an open area of bracken and birch scrub at the top and soon joins a bridlepath, still going due north. When the bridlepath sweeps away left, leave it and follow the narrower path ahead to come to Frithsden Beeches,

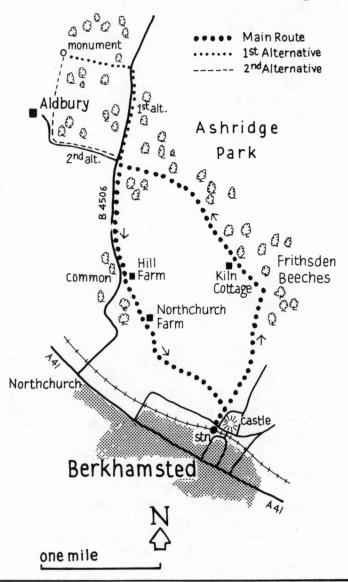

Map 3

Main Route
1st Alternative
2nd Alternative

monument

Aldbury

1st alt.

2nd alt.

Ashridge
Park

B 4506

Hill
Farm

common

Northchurch
Farm

Kiln
Cottage

Frithsden
Beeches

A 41

Northchurch

castle

stn

Berkhamsted

A 41

N

one mile

a heavenly place where, if you are lucky, deer can be seen between the wide-spaced trees. The OS map shows a clear path here leading to the mansion at Ashridge, but even as we set foot upon that path we are halted by a warning sign stating: 'The very old pollarded trees are being retained for their historic interest. They are liable to shed branches, and the public is advised not to enter the area.' The public does, though, as the worn path signifies, doubtless to pass through the grounds of Ashridge Park and turn west on the mile-long avenue leading to the Monument erected in memory of its former owner, Lord Bridgewater. However, I can only advise you to heed the warning notice and turn aside to the narrower FP going left at the notice, keeping roughly west through the bracken to rejoin the bridlepath. But *please* do take the trouble to see the Frithsden Beeches, which are justly famous. Even though you will be walking in woods for much of the day, the wonder and beauty of Frithsden is something you will long remember.

Back at the bridlepath the going is quite foul in places, leading to little diversionary paths having been formed around the worst bits. Cross the paved drive to Kiln Cottage and continue roughly NNW then west as the path takes you, passing Coldharbour and emerging after a mile onto the Northchurch to Ringshall road opposite the Aldbury turn-off.

Here you may make a diversion to the Bridgewater Monument, raised to the third Duke as Father of Inland Navigation (for a brief history of Ashridge and this duke see *Portrait of the Chilterns* in the bibliography) *and the National Trust shop and café, which lie at the top of a broad drive to the west of the road, half a mile north of where you stand. The simplest route is to turn right and follow the road until you come to the drive, but it is also possible to cross and walk some 800 yards along the road towards Aldbury until you come to a clear path on the right striking north uphill to the same destination. The latter is longer, but makes a better walk, being a broad, pleasant path which emerges at the NT shop. Also, the OS map shows an escape route here to the pubs and refreshment places of Aldbury.*

For the return to Berkhamsted, turn south along the Ringshall to Northchurch road and follow it in and out of the trees along the verge, watching out for Hill Farm on the left. Just past this entrance a narrow path goes off through the trees left towards

Northchurch Farm. Do not take the stile here onto the farm lands, but cross the farm road and continue along the bridlepath opposite, downhill, turning right when you reach houses 500 yards ahead. You are now on a hard path; turn left with it and continue to the end, and at the last house an easterly path across fields will take you back downhill all the way to Berkhamsted, passing eventually through a stile at an iron gate to go through a farmyard and emerge at Castle Hill, near your starting place.

Walk 4

Tring station – Bulbourne Junction – Startopsend village – Marsworth village – Wilstone village – Wilstone reservoir – Tringford reservoir – Marsworth reservoir – Startopsend reservoir – Tring station

(9 miles)

ALTERNATIVE
Start and end at Startopsend village
(4½ miles)

OS map 165
Sketch map 4

P Tring station carpark GR 952123
Startopsend GR 919140
Station: Tring BR

Few regular walkers are without some interest in birds or wild flowers, and for such this last walk from Tring station, centred on the nature reserves at Little Tring, Wilstone, Marsworth and Startopsend (or 'Starrupsend', as you will hear it locally), will prove a treat.

These clear marl lakes, fed by natural springs, were dug in the nineteenth century to provide extra water for the Grand Union canal where it crosses the summit of the hills. Though the navigators took the canal through the Tring gap it still makes quite a height, and every time a boat goes over the summit an unbelievable 200,000 gallons flows back down the canal. So side pounds were constructed as feeders at the series of locks between Bulbourne and Marsworth, and when that proved insufficient, these great lakes were excavated.

Today the Tring reservoirs are a world-famous nature reserve and wetland habitat. Take your binoculars to search for the redcrested pochard, little ringed plover and grey shrike and to

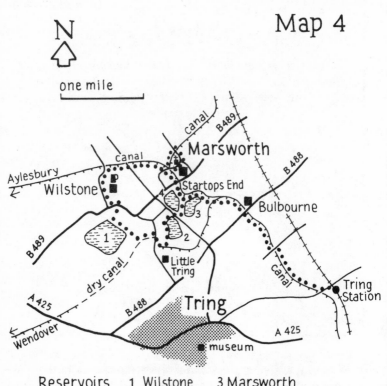

N

one mile

Map 4

Reservoirs
1 Wilstone   3 Marsworth
2 Tringford   4 Startops End

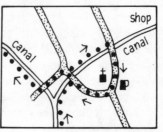

Route through Marsworth

watch the mating dance of great crested grebes. Herons either flapping overhead or brooding on one leg against the reeds, you will spot with the naked eye. Wild flowers abound in season, including many rare species like water figwort, mudwort, and the green flowered helleborine that grows at Wilstone. Winter walkers must sacrifice the flowers in exchange for the thrill of the lapwings calling and the great flocks of wintering birds on the lakes.

To say that this is a 4½ or 9 mile walk along the canal bank, visiting two canalside villages and a nature reserve, belies its great interest and variety. This is a walk which is strongly recommended, and even if you don't think of yourself as a bird watcher, *don't forget your binoculars*! or you'll be kicking yourself all day.

From Tring station, a simple left turn along the road in the direction of Tring will bring you to the bridge over the Grand Union within 100 yards, the towpath being on the nearside. Turn north along the towpath and you will find yourself at the start of a pretty and secluded 1½ mile walk to the Grand Junction Arms at Bulbourne. On this stretch the canal runs through a deep, wooded cutting, haunt of fishermen and lovers of solitude. You won't pass a single lock along here, but once past the Bulbourne Junction, where the Wendover arm goes off to the west, you will come to six locks within half a mile. Soon after this junction, too, you will see the first of the reservoirs, Marsworth, which is separated from Startopsend by such a narrow causeway that they appear to be one great lake. You could be tempted onto this causeway, which you find by leaving the towpath and rising up to the top of the bank, but before you go too far at this stage in the walk, do note that the causeway forms part of the return route. Better to continue along the towpath now until the canalside houses of Startopsend, a National Nature Reserve in the care of the Nature Conservancy Council, come into view ahead. There are two more inns here for refreshment, the White Lion by the bridge or the quieter Anglers' Retreat on the corner of Watery Lane, to the left.

It will be interesting to look out for examples of canal architecture along the way. Victorian terraces such as this one at Startopsend can be found in most of the canalside villages, though sometimes they have been 'improved' almost beyond recognition, and here you will see old iron pumping gear, and warehouses and other wharfside buildings which can be recognized from a uniformity of brickwork and design.

The canal bridge at Startopsend was originally a turnover bridge, where the towpath crosses from one bank to the other; though here the towpath also continues on the left bank to become the towpath to the Aylesbury arm from Marsworth Junction, some 400 yards ahead. Our first destination is Marsworth, so cross here by the footbridge beside the White Lion and follow the towpath on the right-hand bank for half a mile, coming to Marsworth at the second canal bridge. Here to the right of the bridge are the Red Lion and the remains of the old canal village, and to the left of the bridge, on the far bank, are a few thatched cottages and a canal shop and café. Such shops as this were once commonplace along the Cut; today they are a rarity, to be remarked upon and visited.

Our route now goes on through Marsworth village to turn right at the church onto a narrow downhill lane where you will come to two canal bridges in quick succession. Go over the first bridge, which crosses the Grand Union, and bear left to proceed to the second, spanning the narrower Aylesbury arm. Cross this bridge and descend to the towpath on the far side, walking away from the Junction. At any time of year gatherings of bright painted narrowboats can be seen from these bridges, which give a good view of Marsworth Junction and the canal signpost pointing to London, Braunston and Aylesbury.

A long half mile on this Aylesbury arm towpath brings us to Wilstone, another picturesque canalside village and one that was more imaginatively developed than Marsworth in the post-Sixties building boom. On this stretch the locks again come thick and fast, but now they are narrow locks built to the original 7 foot standard. There is a skill to locking through here, and if you don't know what you are about you can find your boat sitting on the bottom! That this arm is in use all the way to Aylesbury boat basin is largely to the credit of the Aylesbury Canal Society, whose members still keep a watching brief.

Leave the towpath at Wilstone (second road bridge from Marsworth Junction) and turn left to walk straight through the village, past the Half Moon, to the T-junction with the B489, which is reached in about 500 yards. Turn right at this junction for a brief 50 yards along a busy road with no footway, to climb the bank of Wilstone reservoir, opposite. Our route goes left along the bank top, though you may wish to spend time looking round first.

Keep left along the south-east bank of the lake until, at trees and a reedbed, you leave it to take the broad path ahead, forking right after a few steps onto a winding path which returns you to the lake shore before going briefly left again to join a wider, grassier way. Turn right here for 100 yards, when you turn sharp left at a 'No Entry' gate onto a narrow footpath between scrub. Soon, with a stile ahead, you will find a broad path crossing with a wide ditch on the far side. This is the dry section of the former Wendover arm, and you turn left here to walk along what is, effectively, the towpath, for another quarter mile to the road.

This Wendover section was another narrow canal like the Aylesbury arm and was, in fact, built first. For some years there was a flourishing trade along here, with extensive wharves at the Wendover terminus in Wharf Road. But the arm was built with a bottom of puddled clay which proved porous; the water steadily drained away and had to be topped up continually, and eventually the decision was taken to allow the section from Little Tring to Buckland Wharf to go dry. The section from Buckland Wharf to Halton was lined with concrete by the Rothschilds to keep the water out of their dining room at Green Park. At the Wendover end the waterway is fed by a natural spring.

As you come to the road (the B489) you can glimpse Tringford reservoir, ahead and slightly to the left. To reach it, turn briefly right along the road towards Little Tring, then left down a sandy road past the manor house to a stile ahead which gives access to the lakeside. The route goes left around the shore here, though again you may wish to explore first.

Returning to the B489, cross and turn right and within a few yards you will find the entrance to Marsworth and Startopsend reservoirs, where you can at last walk along the causeway that separates them, to my mind the high point of the walk.

At the end of the causeway you are back at the Grand Union, where you will turn either right for Tring station *or left for Startopsend*, according to your mode of transport.

2   Walks in the Hills from Wendover

The historic town of Wendover, where records go back to 1214, is one of the best centres for walkers. The town has a dignified antiquity mercifully unspoiled by modern development and is surrounded by woods and high hill country which make for splendid walking. Furthermore, it has a station on the Metropolitan line from Marylebone, good free carparks and toilets, and, at the time of writing, can provide breakfast and a thermos filled at the Station Café, morning coffee at the Bookshop in Aylesbury Road, lunch at any one of half a dozen old inns, and afternoon tea at either of two teashops near the road junction to Great Missenden.

These walks centred on Wendover give a chance for a good look at the old inns and pretty cottages, for no matter which walk you choose it would be a sin to leave the town without taking time to acquaint yourself with its joys, not least of which is the antiques arcade in the old Post Office building in the High Street. In an upstairs room here are some quite remarkable examples of domestic wall paintings.

This walk begins at a stile on the south side of the Ellesborough Road (A4010), GR 862074. This is not the stile almost opposite Wendover station entrance, but another some 400 yards on at a bend where there is off-road parking for four or five small cars. This space is quickly filled up on most days.

Walk 5

Wendover station – Coombe Hill – Butlers Cross – Ellesborough – Pulpit Hill – Plough Inn – Whiteleaf Cross – Princes Risborough

(6 miles)

ALTERNATIVES
Omit Butlers Cross – Ellesborough – Pulpit Hill
(3 miles)
Return to Wendover from Butlers Cross
(4–4½ miles)
Return to Wendover from Pulpit Hill
(6 miles)

OS map 165
Sketch map 5

P Wendover station GR 856078
Library carpark in Wendover High Street GR 868078
Station: Wendover (Met. line from Marylebone)

From this stile your first destination is the Boer War Monument on the north face of Coombe Hill, rather more than a mile away. This was raised to commemorate 148 men of the Buckinghamshire Regiment who died in the Boer War; it is a landmark for miles across the vale and is known locally simply as 'The Monument'. Any of the paths going WSW uphill here will bring you eventually to the Monument, including the Ridgeway LDFP. I suggest you take whichever offers easiest going on the day, reflecting, as you trudge uphill, that this is the route of the annual Wendover Fun Run which takes place every year on the first Saturday in June. The record for the dash from the steps of the NatWest Bank in Wendover High Street, up Coombe Hill, once round the Monument and back down to finish in the carpark at the Shoulder of Mutton was 20 minutes and 54 seconds at the time of writing. Individuals and teams of runners gather every year from all over

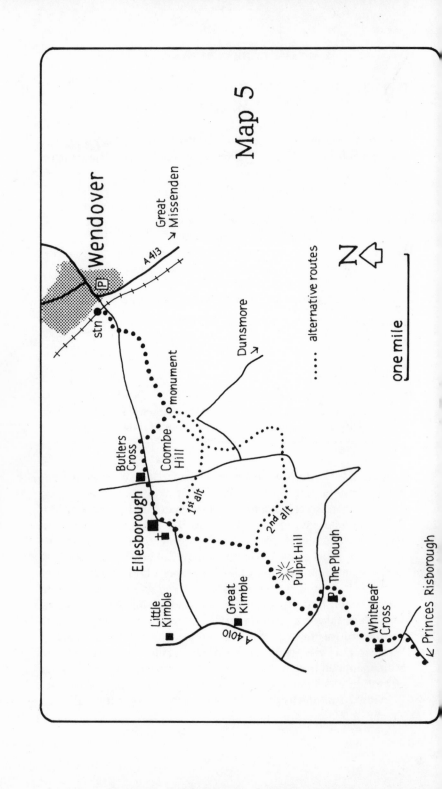

Map 5

the country in an attempt to better this record, and it is a poor year when less than 300 start.

At the Monument the LDFP continues south to strike the road by farm cottages at Buckmoorend and cross the road onto the Prime Minister's land at Chequers. You would have no difficulty following it to the Plough Inn and on to Whiteleaf or Princes Risborough, even without the direction markers kept up by the Countryside Commission, for thousands of pairs of boots have marked the way. It is a shorter route than the one I am about to describe, but very much less enjoyable. So turn north-west instead at the Monument and follow the obvious path downhill to the road by Ellesborough golf course, where a left turn and a brisk downhill walk will bring you to the hamlet of Butlers Cross, the Russell Arms, and a village shop that opens on summer Sundays.

Keeping to the road, carry on over the crossroads and within 500 yards you will come to the tiny village of Ellesborough nestling between the flint and clunch of Ellesborough church to one side and the conical mound of Beacon Hill on the other.

Don't be tempted up the farm road opposite the church unless you want a quick route back to Wendover, when a FP leads off left a little way up the farm road to cross fields to a metalled road and ascend to the Monument which has been in clear sight ahead. This will return you to Wendover after a short walk of some 4–4½ miles.

The true route continues by the stile a few yards to the right of the farm road, which gives onto a green path going gently uphill to another stile at the top. Here it circles the hill to go steeply up between the old gnarled trunks of the famous Kimble box trees. Stick to the path in this short stretch and don't be tempted to wander off into the box trees. If you do, you will rapidly find yourself in an impenetrable thicket stretching from your knees to above your head that you cannot see over, under or through, and your only escape, as mine was when I was once foolish enough to try it, will be to get down and slither downhill below the lowest branches until you emerge from the box wood at the valley bottom. I was saved from my stupidity by the fact that it was a wet day and I was wearing lightweight nylon waterproof anorak and trousers which offered a slippery and impervious surface to the vicious, unyielding branches. I will not try it again.

Eventually the narrow path emerges to cross first a cultivated field and then the paved drive to Chequers before a stile brings you out onto Pulpit Hill. Follow another narrow path right to another stile by a notice telling you that this is a Nature Reserve managed by the Berks, Bucks & Oxfordshire Naturalists' Trust. Once over this stile, take the broadest of the paths before you, bearing left at the top of the rise to circle this hill to yet another stile at the bottom. The broad, muddy path in front of this stile is the Ridgeway LDFP. *Turn left here to return to Wendover*, right to continue on to the Plough Inn, Whiteleaf Cross and Princes Risborough.

Continuing, you should come down fairly steeply to the Cadsden Road within half a mile, to cross the road and go left up the side road opposite for the Plough Inn, which you should reach nicely in time for lunch. In days gone by it was traditional for the landlord's wife here at the Plough to bake a cherry pie every year on June 17th in the shape of a coffin to commemorate the death of John Hampden in the Civil War. His body rested for one night at the Plough as it was carried home from Thame by his Buckinghamshire Greencoats for burial in the family burial ground at Hampden. The men of the Buckinghamshire Regiment were known as The Cherrypickers.

If you miss the south-west turn on Pulpit Hill where the LDFP leaves the obvious way and goes sharply down and up again in a space of 10 yards, you will find yourself coming down not to the Plough but to the Barnard Arms at Great Kimble. In that event it is best to retrace your steps the gentle half mile back to Pulpit Hill and find the proper route again rather than to try to get round to the Plough by road, which is boring and much longer. However, before returning just pop into St Nicholas church to see the historic document headed 'Kimble Magna, Januarie the 8th, 1635' and signed by John Hampden and thirty-one others, formally recording their refusal to pay Ship Money, the illegally applied tax that was a precipitating factor in the Civil War and Hampden's death (see *Portrait of the Chilterns*). It is said the first shots of the Civil War were fired in the churchyard at Great Kimble.

The route onwards follows the LDFP to cross in front of the Plough and go steeply up between the trees on the right until it emerges onto the open hilltop. Whiteleaf Cross is carved into the north face of the hill, overlooking the Oxfordshire Plain. This cross and a similar one on the hillside at Bledlow mark the sides of the Risborough gap, and, like the Monument, they are prominent

Chiltern landmarks. Great antiquity is sometimes claimed for Whiteleaf Cross, but in fact its first mention is in a Charter of 903 where it is mentioned as a boundary mark, and we hear no more of it until George IV's time when an Act of Parliament laid upon the owners of the Hampden estate the responsibility for keeping the outline free from encroaching grass and weeds.

To reach the Cross you simply veer far right across the greensward on the crown of the hill. The Cross itself doesn't look much as you stand beside it, but the view over Oxfordshire on a sunny day is stunning.

Those who plan to return to Wendover could well turn back here. To follow the Ridgeway on to Princes Risborough would do little more than turn a 9 mile walk into a 10 mile one, though there are toilets, restaurants and inns there, and the area around the Market Hall is worth exploring. There is also the thought that any town you haven't seen is worth an extra mile. Walkers who have come out by train from Marylebone could return there from the Chiltern line station at Princes Risborough – a good idea for winter walkers whose days are short.

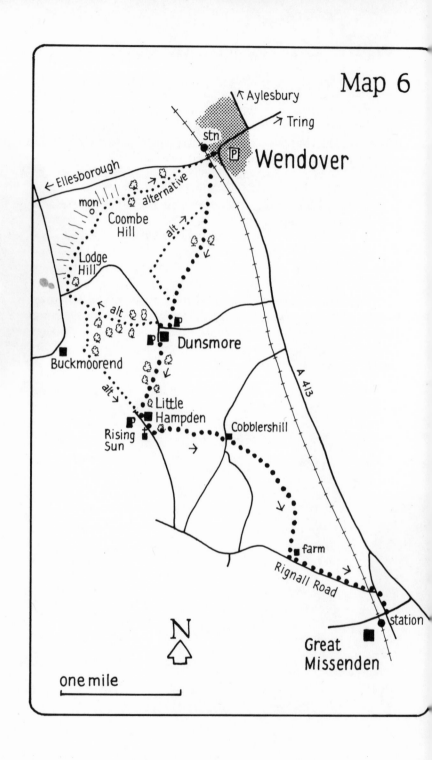

Map 6

Aylesbury
Tring
stn
Wendover
← Ellesborough
mon
alternative
Coombe Hill
alt
Lodge Hill
alt
Buckmoorend
Dunsmore
alt
Little Hampden
Rising Sun
Cobblershill
A 413
farm
Rignall Road
station
N
Great Missenden
one mile

Walk 6

Wendover station – Dunsmore – Buckmoorend – Little Hampden – Lodge Hill – Wendover

(6 miles)

ALTERNATIVES
Wendover – Dunsmore – Wendover
(3 miles)
Wendover – Dunsmore – Lodge Hill – Coombe Hill – Wendover
(4 miles)
Return to Great Missenden station from Little Hampden
(6 miles)

OS map 165
Sketch map 6

[P] Wendover station GR 856078
Library carpark in Wendover High Street GR 868078
Station: Wendover (Met. line from Marylebone)

This next walk is a pleasant amble through woods and farmland. It can be either a 3 mile or 4 mile round walk from Wendover to Dunsmore, a longer 6 mile round walk from Wendover to Little Hampden returning over Lodge Hill, or a straight 6 mile walk from Wendover station to Great Missenden station.

This walk starts at the stile in Ellesborough Road immediately opposite the railway station entrance which earlier in this chapter you were told to ignore. As you leave the station entrance and cross the railway line you see the stile hidden in the hedge almost immediately opposite, giving onto a footpath going due south.

After crossing a cornfield this path emerges in a lane with houses on one side only, where it turns right for 50 yards to an old green iron FP sign in the hedge pointing south along a broad, grassy path between the houses. This is a true country walk, over stiles and through meadow and woodland with birds singing overhead and

wild flowers along the way. In a good year you will see butterflies –
meadow brown and speckled wood among others – and as you
come to farm ponds beside the path there may be vivid darting
dragonflies.

The path continues first south then SSW, ignoring all branches
to left or right, until it is joined by an iron fence coming in from the
right. Soon after this it leaves the shelter of the wood to cross two
fields and come to Dunsmore. You will pass the first pub, The Fox,
in its pretty garden setting, before you reach the crossroads; the
Black Horse lies behind the village hall on a no-through road
beside the pond.

*If a short stroll and a snack was your aim you could return now to
Wendover going back past The Fox onto the path by which you
came, leaving it quite soon where a stile leads left into the woods.
This stile gives onto a footpath bearing first north-west then
north-east, kindly waymarked (probably by the Chiltern Society)
with white arrows on the trees. This will return you after twenty
minutes to half an hour to the path across two cornfields which
brought you out from Wendover. Don't stray too far left into the
woods after making your north-east turn or you will find yourself
mixed up in the point to point course in Bacombe Warren. In fact, if
there is much activity with horses in the wood you might do better to
return to Wendover entirely on the route by which you came,
instead of trying this diversion. Either route gives a round walk of
roughly 3 miles from Wendover to Dunsmore and back.*

To extend your walk, take the road past Dunsmore pond
signposted 'Kimble & Princes Risborough', where a few yards on
you will find a stile beside a farm gate giving onto a path going
south across fields to a distant wood. Here the path takes a brief
left turn behind a farm before continuing SSW for a mile through
the wood to Little Hampden. In bad weather this direct route can
be muddy, so if you are not too well shod you might prefer to
continue at Dunsmore along the Kimble Road to another
woodland path which goes west beside a private road through
Fugsden Wood. This path continues almost due west for some
three-quarters of a mile, ignoring all paths joining or crossing,
until it comes to a junction of several paths. The most obvious and
muddy path (as always) is the Ridgeway LDFP. Here you have a
choice: you can either turn left onto the LDFP to make your way
by another route to Little Hampden as first planned, or *you can*

turn right to come out within half a mile onto Lodge Hill, returning to Wendover via Coombe Hill and the Monument, as described in Walk no. 5.

If you decide for Little Hampden and turn left onto the LDFP, a half mile walk will bring you to farm cottages at Buckmoorend, when you turn up the farm road past the cottages, going first south then east on the hard surface then south again through woodland, to Little Hampden Common, now much overgrown and reduced to a smallish area of bracken. Keep the bracken on your right, and as it ends cross the path ahead to go first left then a few steps right, when you will come out into a clearing beside the Rising Sun at Little Hampden.

'Little' is a true description of this hamlet: a tiny church, a good food pub, Manor Farm and a handful of houses cluster together where a no-through road, itself no more than a winding lane, ends in beech woods. But peace and quietness abound, and the medieval church a little way along the lane has an unusual timber-framed two-storey porch and faded wall-paintings of the Weighing of Souls.

As an alternative to returning to Wendover via Buckmoorend and Lodge Hill, you could go on 3 miles from Little Hampden to Great Missenden, which is the station before Wendover on the Metropolitan Line, either returning home from there or taking the train back to your car at Wendover.

This alternative route goes via the footpath going east through the woods and across fields to Cobblers Hill, a short mile distant. There are several paths going east into the woods here, you need neither the one right at the end of the lane, nor the bridlepath past Manor Farm, but the FP which enters the wood via a five-barred gate opposite a broad lane junction on the right, just before the church. This path goes east, briefly south, then east again to emerge at Cobblers Hill immediately opposite the broad farm road which goes due south-east for a good 1½ miles to emerge onto the road by Rignall Farm. Bear right at the halfway fork; if you find yourself going under the railway line you have missed this right fork and must go back to it.

Arriving at Rignall Farm, turn east into Rignall Road, that is to pass the farm and farm cottages, when you will come to Gt Missenden in little more than a mile.

Walk 7

Wendover station – nature reserve – Weston Turville – Halton – Buckland Wharf – Wendover

(10 miles)

ALTERNATIVES
Wendover – Weston Turville – Wendover
(5 miles)
Wendover – Weston Turville – Halton – Wendover
(6½ miles)

OS map 165
Sketch map 7

P Wendover station GR 856078
Library carpark in Wendover High Street GR 868078
Station: Wendover (Met. line from Marylebone)

This canal walk from Wendover to Buckland Wharf and back will appeal to souls with a liking for damp, lonely places, isolated from the world and with no sound save for the skylarks in the cornfields, the stirring of the breeze in the trees and the soft flowing water. The principal attraction is the nature reserve at Weston Turville reservoir, in the care of the Berks, Bucks & Oxfordshire Naturalists' Trust, where you may see up to forty-six species of breeding birds, including the North American ruddy duck, naturalized here after escaping from wildfowl collections in the 1950s. There are also large numbers of winter migrants, and the reservoir is an important wintering site for shovellers and renowned as an autumn roosting place for swallows and martins.

Interest is added by architecture, for this is another walk where the start takes you along Wendover's broad High Street, past the undulating red roof of the Two Brewers which still has its original seventeenth-century tiles, past the Elizabethan King's Head and the half-timbered Red Lion, and into the gracious tree-lined

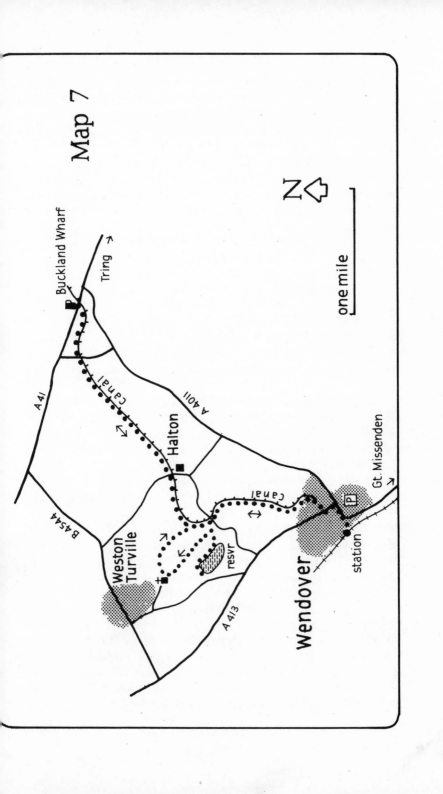

Map 7

Aylesbury Road, where the bonnet of a well-preserved windmill can be seen rising beyond the rows of stately houses. Later there are Rothschild villas at Halton and the thirteenth-century church and Georgian manor house at Weston Turville, all connected by an easy, level walk along the towpath of the Wendover arm of the Grand Union Canal.

Do remember your binoculars for this one, and if you are walking in high summer you might like to remember insect repellent too. The midges along this reedy and tree-hung section are fierce.

From Wendover station entrance, or from the carpark, turn into Wendover High Street and make up towards the nineteenth-century clocktower, where you turn left into Aylesbury Road. Here lovely buildings stretch in an unbroken line: Corner House, The Old House, and Chiltern House (all eighteenth-century) and The Grange (seventeenth-century, according to Pevsner), while the Temperance Hotel is part sixteenth-century. Continue along here for some 500 yards to where Wharf Road goes off on the right, and walk along Wharf Road until, as you come to the school, a narrow lane leads left to the start of the Wendover arm.

There was indeed a wharf here, until the arm was closed in 1904; there was also a boat basin complete with wharfside buildings and a winding eye for turning the 70 foot narrow boats. Now it is just a wide, weed-choked backwater with a freshwater stream welling up into the shallow bed. Unfortunately this arm of the canal was never satisfactory; it was built originally as a feeder to the main canal, but its bed was porous and instead of helping to top up the main channel the arm was continually draining the precious water away. Eventually the stretch between Buckland Wharf and the Tringford pumping station was allowed to go dry. But for that we might still see a boat basin here at Wendover as we do at Aylesbury, with moorings for the brightly painted narrow boats that make such interesting homes and leisure craft.

After an uneventful mile along the grassy towpath away from Wendover a bridge crosses the canal carrying the road from Worlds End to Halton. *Walkers who wish to see Weston Turville church and visit The Chequers without seeing the nature reserve, should continue on along the canal for another 200 yards past the exit at the first road bridge, when a path will be found going up the bank to the left where the copse ends at a cornfield. The footpath is not (at the time of writing) signposted, but it crosses the cornfield, keeping to the nearside of the hedge, north-westerly for half a mile, before taking a left (west) turn to cross a stile where the hedge ends and making straight across the cornfield for Weston Turville church. You will see the church as you begin your walk through the poppies and cornflowers, only to lose it as the land swells between. It remains hidden, then, until you come to the stile giving onto the final meadow, when it appears again to guide you across.*

Walkers wishing to see the nature reserve should leave the canal here at the iron gate under the bridge. There are two footpaths here, one going off right into the copse and the other following the road; keep to the latter as it wends beside the road for a short distance south-westerly. Where it comes down to the carriageway a FP sign points right (north-west) beside a pleasant house. There is a story to this house, Perch Cottage, for which I am indebted to the present owner. It seems that until the late 1800s there was a thatched pub on this site, called the Golden Perch. One of the Rothschilds, probably Lord Alfred, who owned Halton, acquired the land when the Golden Perch burnt down and built the present house as a gamekeeper's cottage. One has but to look at this substantial villa to understand how well the Rothschilds treated their employees and why they were held in such high regard locally.

Of particular interest at Perch Cottage are the frescoes depicting rural scenes. You will see more of these frescoes later on the walls of the houses in Halton village.

But for now we are on the way to the reservoir. Turn up past Perch Cottage for 100 yards or so, when you will be confronted by a field path ahead with a notice saying 'Landowners welcome careful walkers' (and walkers appreciate landowners who leave good, grassy field paths). You will need this path later; now we are going through the gate on the left that gives access to the nature reserve. The reservoir is leased out for sailing; our path goes right past the clubhouse and the beached boats with the wind slapping in their rigging, and continues through the rough woodland that goes down to the water's edge. As with all water margins, the going can be muddy and you will need good boots.

Stick to the main path, ignoring the short tracks on the left that lead to fishermen's stations, and soon you will be skirting the reservoir along the bank top with a clear view across the water on your left and Weston Turville church across the fields on your right. The sight of multitudes of birds on water is always thrilling, though often enough the bright white dots that catch the eye are only seagulls and we must look more carefully for the duller but more interesting species.

Unfortunately it is not, at the time of writing, possible to walk right round the lake. The path along the bank top leads only to the parking place off the A413 at GR 858097, so we must return towards Perch Cottage, to the field path to Weston Turville where the landowners welcome us. We are making for Weston Turville church; our first sight of it is the flagpole appearing over the horizon, followed by the church tower and the buildings of Church Farm. Our field path brings us to a stile by a five-barred gate. Once over the stile the instinct is to bear right towards the farm, but that is not the way. Instead the path continues ahead, crossing the field towards a white-painted dovecote, when it keeps beside the fence to come onto the road at a kissing gate.

This is Church End, Weston Turville; our way goes on through the churchyard, but if you feel it is time for refreshments turn left up the lane instead for 100 yards, then right at the end, when another 100 yards or so through the modern estate will bring you to old Weston Turville, thatched cottages and a country pub, the Aylesbury Brewery Co.'s Chequers Inn. The Chequers has a separate restaurant, but also does good bar snacks and has tables outside.

Either before or after the break you will want to look at St Mary's Church, thirteenth-century flint and rubble with a lovely churchyard full of flowers. St Mary's was restored in 1963 by a local firm, Wrights of Great Missenden, under the direction of J.H. Cox. The restoration was delicately done; all the best bits were preserved and the church remains humble, workworn and holy.

Walk through the churchyard to the FP at the back which crosses the meadow ahead. The route of this path is not always clear; the map marks it going due east for 500 yards then SSE a similar distance, but if the meadow is not cultivated and there is no obvious path, make towards the top left-hand corner where you will find a stile giving onto another path going sharp right on the nearside of the hedge. This path will return you to the Wendover arm, a short mile from the church.

As you cross the fields here you will get a good view of the towers and curlicues of Halton House, away on your left. Halton was built in the style of a French chateau, similar to Waddesdon but nothing like so extensive, by Baron Alfred de Rothschild. It is not open to the public, so get out your binoculars as this is one of the best views you will get of it. If the RAF ever abandons the House it might be a different story.

Back on the canal towpath, we have the choice of *turning south and returning to Wendover*, or taking a left turn to continue half a mile NNE to Halton, where we will find Halton village at the next road bridge. Halton village, as distinct from the buildings connected with RAF Halton, is worth a mile of anybody's time. At first sight, as you climb up from the towpath, the half-timbered houses look truly old; one building even has the semi-circular bulge of a bread oven or smoke hole built out from the chimney breast. In fact we owe it all to Baron Alfred, whose family built extensively in this 'Jacobethan' style, as it is called, all over the Chilterns in the late nineteenth century. They built these 'villas' for their workpeople and 'hunting lodges' for their many guests, of which the Five Arrows at Waddesdon and the Rose & Crown at Tring are examples. The use to which their hunting lodges were put would have dismayed the Rothschilds, who disapproved of public houses – witness the building of a gamekeeper's lodge on the site of the old Golden Perch.

The Rothschild villas, large and small, have survived well, and it is interesting to spot them as you go about the Chilterns. These houses at Halton are particularly fine, with the Rothschild crest and motto on many of them and some with frescoes high on the walls depicting the occupations of the workers they were built for: the woodman's house, the herdsman's house, the farm bailiff's house, etc. But there is no pub. The Rothschilds were content to leave it to the impoverished English aristocracy to patronize the pubs: the Marquis of Granby, the Sir Francis Drake, the Bedford Arms ...

The Wendover arm goes on a long 1½ miles from Halton to where the New Inn on the A41 has been renamed the Buckland Wharf. This is another place for refreshment, with a row of pretty canal cottages to one side and a grassy garden onto the canal on the other. Half a mile past Halton village the towpath crosses to the other bank, possibly to preserve the privacy of Green Park, another former Rothschild estate, now owned by the County. The canal bed was lined with concrete here to cure it of the nasty habit of emptying itself into the Green Park dining room, an expediency which might have saved the whole arm had it belonged to the Rothschilds instead of to the impoverished Grand Union Canal Company. When you see the last of Green Park, you have only another half mile to go to Buckland Wharf. Once there, you should retrace your steps.

Wendover Woods

North and east from Wendover the view is of high, inviting woodland crowning the ridge. This is principally the mass of Wendover Woods, most of which is in the charge of the Forestry Commission. The Commission's wardens have created a fine leisure area here, with a horse trail and four walkers' trails: Aston Hill Ramble, Hale View and Beech Hangings, all a mile and a half long, and Boddington Banks which is three-quarters of a mile. In addition there is Daniel's Trudge, another mile and a half, in Aston Hill Coppice.

These mileages are a guide only for car drivers, who can enter either the woods or the coppice from Aston Hill, north-east of Wendover at GR 892100 off the A4011 road to Tring, where Aston Hill Coppice is to the left of the road and the entrance to Wendover Woods to the right. A map of the walks is obtainable from the Forestry Commission office on the A4011, at GR 885104, but you can manage without as you will find wayfaring stations in the carparks. You will find yourself driving a good mile from the entrance into the woods before you come to the main picnic site and wayfaring station.

Walkers from Wendover station can enter the woods by a footpath, known locally as the Snake, at the south-west corner. Make up Wendover High Street to the clocktower, then veer round left into the Tring road. Keep to the right-hand pavement, and after some 300 yards a footpath sign points you up right between houses. Turn left at the top of the path, and soon you will come to a sandy lane going east between hedgerows. At the top of this lane a narrow FP goes uphill right to a stile at the top which gives access to the woods.

Cross the bridlepath and take the FP ahead, still going east, by a 'No horses' sign. A stiff, but pleasant, climb here will bring you to a broad pathway at the top, which is actually part of the Boddington Banks trail, waymarked with arrows on a white ground. Unless you want to follow this trail, turn left to leave the area by the road gate, when you will find yourself by the turning circle at the end of the permitted car road. Half a mile up the sandy road ahead you will find the main picnic area, toilet, and waymarking station. Also up this sandy road, a little past the turning circle, you will find the start of Beech Hangings trail, waymarked in yellow.

At the end of the Beech Hangings trail you come to the blue markings of Aston Hill Ramble, where you can turn right for the main picnic area and waymarking station, or left to follow the Ramble for a mile to join the car road. Turn left to follow this road for 500 yards and you will come to the entrance at Aston Hill, where you will find the entrance to Daniel's Trudge on the opposite side of Aston Hill.

Now for some mileages: it is roughly 2 miles from Wendover station to the turning circle, another 1½ miles to Beech Hangings, and a further 1½ miles to Aston Hill Ramble, making a total of 5 miles, or 10 miles if you make it a round trip from Wendover station and back (or 11½ miles if you add in Daniel's Trudge). It is a long walk, if you take it all in one, and you'll be glad it's down hill most of the way back.

These woods are a joy at all seasons, and the waymarked walks take you through the best of them. Part of the area has been planted with pine but much of it is good mixed woodland, and nowhere does it present the silent and lifeless appearance we have come to associate with commercial planting. In places the views are very fine, as at Hale View. Above Halton you can see the steep, leaded roofs of Halton Towers, the miniature Waddesdon built for Lord Alfred de Rothschild which is now the Officers' Mess at RAF Halton. Lord Alfred, who owned all this woodland, cut down his trees for pit props in the First World War and gave Halton to the nation for the duration. It was occupied by the War Ministry, and when Lord Alfred died in 1918 the Government decided to purchase the whole estate.

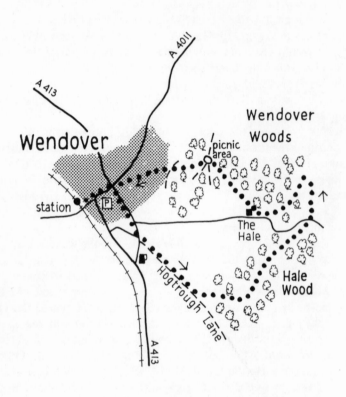

Map 8

A 4011

A 413

Wendover

Wendover
Woods

picnic
area

station

P

The
Hale

Hogtrough Lane

Hale
Wood

A 413

N

one mile

Walk 8

Wendover station – Hogtrough Lane – Barn Wood – Hale Wood – The Hale – Wendover Woods – Wendover

(8 miles)

OS map 165
Sketch map 8

P Wendover station GR 856078
Library carpark in Wendover High Street GR 868078
Station: Wendover (Met. line from Marylebone)

This next round walk from Wendover station takes in part of Wendover Woods, and part of Hale Wood. You will find it one of the best short walks in the book.

Turn left from Wendover station or right from the carpark along Wendover High Street towards the clocktower, where a footpath sign points you right along Heron Path towards the parish church. Keep along here between houses and stream, ignoring the inviting bridges across the water, to St Mary's, where the route skirts the church to go left along Church Lane. At the end of this lane you come to a fastish road, where the Wellhead Inn is a little to your right opposite.

Cross the road to proceed up Hogtrough Lane opposite, and keep to this south-easterly path as it becomes a rougher track until, after a short mile, a Ridgeway LDFP sign points you left into woodland. Follow the LDFP here through Barn Wood and Hale Wood, skirting Cocks Hill, until it comes to the road by Uphill Farm. This walk through high, mixed woodland is one of the better stretches of the Ridgeway Path.

At Uphill, follow the LDFP signs across the lane to enter woodland again opposite, staying with the path until it turns sharply right at a deep crossing ditch. Leave the LDFP here, turning left instead to follow the ditch westwards for a scant half mile until you emerge onto the road again at The Hale, a pretty hamlet with a farmhouse and a manor house along the road to the left. Care needs to be taken on the narrow path along the ditch bottom, where large flints and old, slippery branches are hidden under a thick carpet of leaves. I walk here because I like it, but you may prefer to climb the steep bank and find a pathway along the top.

When you reach The Hale, ignore the obvious FP signposted back across the greensward on your right, and walk right along the lane instead, westwards for 200 yards to a forestry path by another house, where another FP sign points you up to a gate back into Wendover Woods. These woods, which are extensive, are criss-crossed with paths, not only the waymarked trails and bridle paths, but roads and temporary tracks used by Forestry Commission workers and plain, unmarked green tracks and footpaths. Care is needed if you are not to lose your way, so follow the instructions closely.

You will enter the woods on a broad, hard track; *keep to this track*, ignoring all paths off, as it goes north then north-west for a good mile to emerge by a road gate at the turning circle marking the end of the permitted car road through the woods. Half a mile up the sandy road to the right here is the main carpark and picnic area, so if you *do* lose your way try to make for this picnic area, from which you can turn south along the sandy path to the turning circle.

For the route back to Wendover, go through the road gate a few steps left of the gate through which you have emerged, and as you enter the woods again you find another broad path before you. A few yards along here on the right a footpath goes steeply west down through the trees to a bridlepath at the bottom. Cross this bridlepath to leave the woods finally at the stile a few yards ahead.

Here you emerge onto a sandy roadway which will bring you in a short while to an estate of modest houses. Soon you will find a narrow walkway between the houses on the right down to the A4011 Tring road. Turn left along Tring Road for an easy half mile downhill back to Wendover.

3 *Walks in the Hills from Princes Risborough*

The walks in this group centre on Princes Risborough, a medieval market town that takes its first name from the Black Prince who 'acquired' it from the Earl of Cornwall, while Monks Risborough next door was once owned by the monks of Canterbury Cathedral. The 'Risborough', we are assured, is derived from 'Hrisebyrgan be Chilternes estes', or 'Brushwood by the Chiltern eaves'.

If you can spare the time at the beginning or end of one of the walks to wander around the old parts of either town, you will be well rewarded. Make for the Market Square at Princes Risborough, then turn down Church Street for the church and manor house and walk north through the back streets to Monks Risborough and the old church there. You will find a wealth of thatched cottages in pretty gardens set along narrow lanes and walkways – the very fabric of old England.

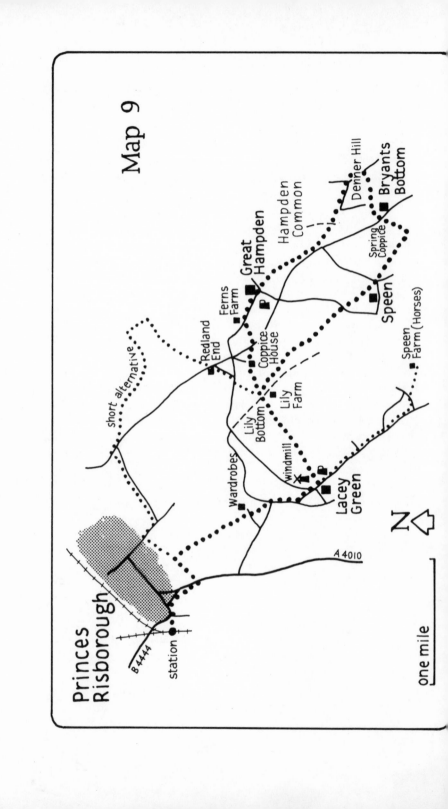

Walk 9

Princes Risborough station – Wardrobes – Lacey Green – Lily Bottom – Speen – Bryants Bottom – Hampden Row – Great Hampden – Keepershill Wood – Princes Risborough

(12 miles)

ALTERNATIVES
Return to Princes Risborough from Lily Bottom via Redland End – Green Hailey – Risborough Kop
(7½ miles)

Visit Speen farm (2½ miles extra)

OS map 165
Sketch map 9

P Public carpark in Princes Risborough GR 824036
Station: Princes Risborough BR

This first walk starts from Princes Risborough station on the Chiltern line from Marylebone. Starting out along the Upper Icknield Way, it goes by meadow and woodland, hill and valley bottom, showing the Chiltern countryside at its remote best. This is no walk for people who dislike stiles, and dogs will often need to be on a lead. But there is a chance to see the restored windmill at Lacey Green and the Home of Rest for Horses at Speen Farm.

Turn left from the station entrance, then right up to Summerleys Road. Turn right again here for 50 yards to bear left with the road and turn right along Poppy Road to the Black Prince Hotel at the top. Bear right again here to pass the Risborough garage and cross the main Wycombe road to where, within 200 yards, the Upper Icknield Way goes off on the left.

After 500 yards or so along the Icknield Way there is a crossing track, where the route goes right over a stile to follow the FP a good mile SSE, keeping beside a fence to descend the wooded dip at Pyrtle Spring then rise to a stile, top left. Still SSE, it crosses the drive to Wardrobes, a large house on the left where there has been a house of this name since the fourteenth century.

After crossing Wardrobes, the way goes left again over a stile then bears right diagonally across a meadow to a second stile, still continuing roughly on the same SSE course, to emerge on the road at the junction of Wardrobes Lane and Woodway. Now there is half a mile uphill along Woodway to the Whip Inn at Loosley Row crossroads.

At the far side of the Whip a farm road leads to Lacey Green windmill, a smock mill brought here from Chesham in 1821. This mill was in ruins when, in 1969, members of the Historic Works & Buildings group of the Chiltern Society decided to take it in hand. Starting in 1971 with a sagging wreck, to quote from Vol.II of *The Chiltern Society's Story*, 'a Bank Manager, two teachers, a lecturer, a television technician, an ex cocoa buyer, a bridge designer, not to mention the Deputy Director of Telecommunications at the Post Office' restored this mill, working every weekend and in all weathers for ten years. Seeking to 'retain the thumbprint of the men who made it ... nearly 300 years ago' they preserved every piece of timber and machinery in any way capable of preservation, going to endless pains to patch and restore instead of taking the easy way and building up again from new, with the fine result you see today. The windmill is open to the public on summer Sundays and Bank Holidays.

This path beside the Whip is open only for the purpose of visiting the windmill; our path goes off in the same direction a few yards on at a stile beside the bus shelter, north-east across fields towards Lily Bottom Lane, *but there is the option here for a diversion to the Home of Rest for Horses, at Speen Farm, a short 2 miles along the road from the Whip in the direction of Walters Ash; it is interesting to all, but particularly to children.*

This charity was founded in 1886 by a friend of the author of Black Beauty *to provide rest, retirement or convalescence for working horses. Over the years the Home has moved from its original site at Neasden in north-west London first to Cricklewood, then to Boreham Wood, then finally, in 1971, to Speen Farm, where every year something in the region of 200 horses, ponies and donkeys are given rest and skilled care or a loving home in their old age. The Home is open daily (except Thursdays) from 2pm to 4pm. If you intend to visit, send an SAE first to the Secretary, Home of*

Rest for Horses, Speen Farm, Slad Lane, near Lacey Green, Bucks, HP17 0PP, from whom you will receive a useful explanatory leaflet.

Speen Farm is situated at GR 835994 on OS 165. Slad Lane turns left just a mile along the lane past the Whip, from where there is little more than another half mile to the Home.

At 4½ miles each way from Princes Risborough a visit to this Home, combined with a tour of Lacey Green windmill, would make a memorable outing for a summer's day.

The path to Lily Bottom Lane crosses four stiles before bearing right to an iron gate in the corner of a meadow. Through the gate it keeps north-east, and where the fence on the right ends it passes through a gap in the hedge to cross the field ahead, bearing right along the hedge at the far side to another stile. Over this stile it bears diagonally right to one more stile before turning left onto a bridleway through trees which brings it down to the lane at Lily Bank Farm.

Here you may decide to return to Princes Risborough by the short route through Redland End and Green Hailey rather than continue on the 12 mile walk to Speen and Hampden. With Lily Bank Farm behind you, cross the lane to take up the FP to the left of the cottage opposite, keeping left at the fork to pass through a gate and follow the line of Grim's Ditch north-east through the plantation for 500 yards until it emerges onto a road. Our route crosses this road to continue NNE along a lane to the hamlet of Redland End, but if, instead, you turn left here and follow the road for half a mile, you will come to the Pink & Lily, a free house at the junction of Pink Hill and Lily Bottom Lane. This inn can also be reached by turning left along the lane at Lily Bottom Farm.

At Redland End, turn left a few yards at the road junction to cross and go right through a gap and over another stile into Kingsfield Wood, where the route again follows the line of Grim's Ditch, NNE (that same Grim's Ditch mentioned in walk no. 2 from Tring). After a good half mile the ditch makes a sharp right-angle to enclose the Hampden Estate. Bear slightly right here, then left at the fork for 200 yards or so to leave the wood at another stile. Keeping NNE around the edge of the wood until a track crosses from a copse on the right, turn left onto the track and follow it north-west for half a mile through Sergeant's Wood, ignoring all crossing tracks, until it leaves the wood again at a gate by Solinger Farm.

Continue now in roughly the same direction for 400 yards or so along a fenced bridleway, bearing left at the fork, to come to a farm road which will bring you to the public road at Green Hailey. Turn right along the road for 200 yards to a junction, where the left fork takes you up over Risborough Kop then descends to Brimmer Road. A right-hand turn along Brimmer Road for a short distance returns you to the Upper Icknield Way, which you follow south-westerly back to the Black Prince for Poppy Road and Risborough station.

If you can't face the climb over Kop hill at the end of your walk, take the right-hand fork around the lower slopes, which leads you sooner to the Upper Icknield Way, which you can then follow to Brimmer Road and thence to the Black Prince as directed.

For the long walk, then, cross the lane at Lily Bottom Farm to take up the FP on the left of the cottage opposite, bearing right on a south-easterly path (the most right of the three paths confronting you). This path follows the boundary of Monkton Wood for the best part of a mile, always south-easterly, to come to the road at a thatched cottage on the outskirts of Speen. If needing refreshment you could turn right (south) here for a short distance along the road to the village, but the true route crosses here to continue south-east along the rough track of Coleheath Bottom and come to the road again within half a mile.

Turn left along this road for 100 yards only, then left again up Spring Coppice Road, to go right almost immediately over the stile, where an uphill path leads south-east to another stile at the top. Go over this second stile, and diagonally left across the meadow to a third stile in the far corner which gives onto another track bearing SSE. Soon you will have a fine view across North Dean, and, as this view comes into sight, a pair of footpaths leaves the track on the left, one going south-east and the other north-east. Take the left-hand (north-east) path, to cross a stile at an iron gate and on over the meadow towards a house ahead. At the next stile bear right along the drive, away from the house, to negotiate a cattle grid, and take up the path again into the wood opposite. This path bears slightly left, keeping the wood on the right, and goes sharply downhill to the road, giving a good view of Bryants Bottom ahead.

Turn left to go briefly along the road to an (at the time of writing) unmarked path on the right, facing the bus stop, which goes steeply uphill, at first beside houses, to Denner Hill Farm, where it goes left through the farmyard to come to the road beside a cottage. Turn left (NNW) along this road, and left again when the road forks, a good half mile in all, until after a stretch between hedges you come to a wooden gate on your right onto Hampden Common. Go left when the path forks to continue NNW for a short half mile to an asphalt path where you turn right briefly, then left onto a plain path which will bring you to a farm drive and thence to the road.

Turn left again along this road to pass through the tiny village of Hampden Row and on along the lane, now skirting Hampden Common, for another ½ mile to the Hampden Arms at Great Hampden. On leaving the Hampden Arms, go left again briefly along the road towards Speen and Loosley Row, leaving the road to go right (west) at a fork, along the lane for 800 yards to Ferns Farm. Opposite Ferns Farm a FP on the left crosses a stile into Heepershill Wood. Keep to the left-hand path here to go due west, first through pines and then through beeches, to come to another road at yet another stile. Go briefly right along here, until one more stile gives entry to the wood opposite. Here a path bears right on a winding uphill path, still roughly west, to a clearing, where it crosses the drive to Coppice House. Once across this drive, a rough track curves down left to a fork. Take the right-hand path at this fork to go through scrub to the wooden gate in the far right-hand corner, and return to the road again at Lily Bank Farm.

From here you can return to Princes Risborough either on the original route or by following the directions for the shorter walk.

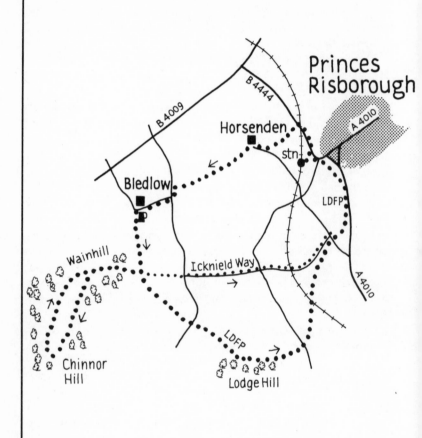

Map 10

Princes
Risborough

B 4444

B 4009

Horsenden

stn

Bledlow

LDFP

Wainhill

Icknield Way

A 4010

LDFP

Chinnor
Hill

Lodge Hill

N

one mile

Walk 10

**Princes Risborough station – Horsenden – Bledlow – Wainhill –
Chinnor Hill – Ridgeway LDFP – Princes Risborough**

(10 miles)

ALTERNATIVE
Return from Chinnor Hill along Icknield Way
(8 miles)

OS map 165
Sketch map 10

P Public carpark in Princes Risborough GR 824036
Station: Princes Risborough BR

The second walk from Princes Risborough station is quite different
from the first, giving the option of a fine ridge walk in place of the
patchwork of woods and fields encountered before. Again the start
is Princes Risborough station, but this time we turn east towards
Bledlow and Wainhill and a superb view across the Oxfordshire
plain.

From Princes Risborough station turn right to walk up to the
B4444, then turn left for a short half mile along the road to a
signposted FP on the left. After 300 yards or so along this metalled
path a stile gives onto a FP ahead, south-west across a meadow,
which will bring you, via the drive to Gate Cottage, to the tiny
hamlet of Horsenden. This path was the direct route to Oxford in
the days when travellers went on foot or on horseback; now only
the power cables go that way, leaving Horsenden blessedly
isolated amid the trees, its few picturesque houses and its
part-fifteenth-century flint church untroubled by passing traffic.

Turn right towards the church to take a WSW footpath opposite
the churchyard gates and follow it over a stile and under the power
cables, then beside a hedge and through a small copse until it
brings you, after a very pleasant mile and several more stiles, onto

a rough track which eventually emerges onto the road at Bledlow (not to be confused with Bledlow Ridge, which is a good 4 miles to the south as the crow flies).

Turn left onto the road at Bledlow, then right after a few yards to proceed along the main road through Bledlow village (though 'main road' is no correct description for such a pleasant byway). Bledlow is one of those memorable villages that even walkers come upon but rarely. The church, set on a mound, is a treasure house: Norman font, fourteenth-century porch, thirteenth-century tower, wall-paintings, stiff leaf capitals to the arcades and a fine eighteenth-century reredos by John Gwynn, and in the porch a commemorative plaque to the ringers who in 1921 rang a 'Peal of Doubles, 5040 changes, being 3,600 of Grandsire and 1,440 of Bob'. One would walk a long way to see Bledlow if the church were all, but in addition there are thatched cottages, their timber frames infilled with tiny Tudor bricks in herringbone; a farm, and an eighteenth-century manor house with a fine weatherboarded barn. There is also a pub, the Lions of Bledlow, in what must be one of the best settings in Buckinghamshire.

Make your way to the Lions at the west end of the village and take the signposted FP going due south across fields. After 500 yards the path is joined by a bridleway coming in from the left. Now it continues as a rough track until, a mile from the Lions, it goes through a gate to a cluster of signposts ahead, among which is the familiar Ridgeway sign; note these signposts for your return. For now, take the most right-hand of the footpaths (which goes to the village of Wainhill) for 500 yards to pass a house close to the path and come to a bridlepath crossing. Bear left onto this bridlepath to climb up around the edge of Bledlow Great Wood to Chinnor Hill. This is an easy path to follow, being a classic hollow way with steep, tree-crowned banks on either hand. It is worth pausing occasionally to look back at the splendid view; the even more splendid view hidden on your right will spread out gloriously before you on the return journey.

After a mile or so you pass a house on the right and the path opens out into a little green. Bear left across the few yards of green to enter the wood again at the path in front of you: not the bridlepath, but the smaller, unmarked FP to the left of it. You will be walking in this wood for about a quarter of a mile until it thins out and you find yourself with springy turf underfoot. Now you have the best before you – a downhill walk around the side of Wainhill back to the cluster of signs noted earlier in the walk, with magnificent views all the way. The track winds about in and out of copses and over turf in a generally northerly direction. Keep well to the left, ignoring all tracks coming in from the right. Towards the end the ground becomes rough and broken, though still green under foot, until the path splits into a footpath which keeps to the ridge and a bridlepath 10 feet below in the hollow. The ways run together; either will return you to the signposts noted earlier. Here you can decide whether to follow the LDFP over Lodge Hill back to Princes Risborough (more pleasant but a distance of 4 miles), *or to take the direct 2 mile route back via the Icknield Way.* Either route will take you across the railway line to emerge onto the A4010, where you should turn left and follow the road into the town, bearing left at the Black Prince for the railway station.

Walk 11

Saunderton station – Bradenham – West Wycombe – Hearnton Wood – Slough Hill – Saunderton

(8 miles)

ALTERNATIVE
Bradenham – West Wycombe – Bradenham
(5 miles)

OS maps 165 and 175
Sketch map 11

P Bradenham village, beside green GR 827972
Station: Saunderton BR

Saunderton seems an odd choice of name for the stop between High Wycombe and Princes Risborough, as the station is closer to Bledlow Ridge or Bradenham. However, Saunderton it is, and this stop is the gateway to many good walks including these routes to West Wycombe (11) and Hughenden Manor (12).

From Saunderton station turn left (east) towards the A4010 and proceed south along the wide verge of this fairly busy road for rather more than a mile to where the Red Lion marks the approach to Bradenham. Turn left for Bradenham village, which you will want to explore.

This little gem is now in the care of the National Trust, and, as always with NT properties, the care and conservation shows. The flint and stone church was restored by the Victorians, and they preserved the best of 700 years of history including the bells cast in the reign of Edward I; the Norman south doorway remains, too. Bradenham Manor, Disraeli's boyhood home, can be seen through the ornamental gateway, and if you are lucky there will be cricket on the village green.

For the route to West Wycombe, skirt the green to the right as you enter the village and take the gravelled path that goes behind

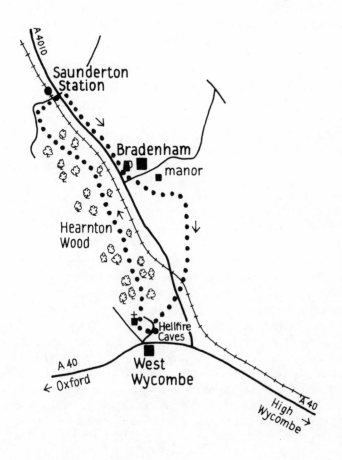

Map 11

A4010

Saunderton
Station

Bradenham

manor

Hearnton
Wood

Hellfire
Caves

A 40

← Oxford

West
Wycombe

A 40

High
Wycombe →

N

one mile

the manor house. After a short distance the track splits and the narrower path to West Wycombe goes off sharp right into woodland (while the broader path ahead leads on to Naphill), winding east, then south-east, then due south for about 1½ miles, when the clear path turns south-west leading to steps down to cross the railway line and the A4010. Then, keeping south-westerly, the path goes diagonally uphill across a meadow and into trees to emerge at West Wycombe.

The village, which was bought in its entirely from the Dashwood family by the Royal Society of Arts in 1929 and given to the National Trust so that it might be preserved as a true example of the English village, lies to your left. Do visit it while you have the chance, or you will kick yourself when you realize what you have missed: jettied upper stories, Queen Anne windows, Regency stucco; old inns; Victorian shop fronts; a fifteenth-century church loft with weathervane and clock. Only two new houses have been built in West Wycombe this century, and one of those is the new vicarage built in 1967. The place is a joy.

More immediately before you is West Wycombe House, the Dashwood mausoleum, and the church of St Laurence with its great golden ball. Footpaths lead up the hill to the church and mausoleum, and the broad hilltop makes a perfect picnic spot, with views across the rolling countryside.

If you have parked at Bradenham you should return there the same way, but for the main route back to Saunderton station, cross the hilltop from the church towards the car exit, then turn left along the lane a short distance to Windyhaugh House. Keep to this same north-westerly track as it goes in and out of Hearnton Wood for the best part of 3½ miles, ignoring all turnings off, until it comes at last to a paved lane at the foot of Slough Hill. Turn right here, and Saunderton station will be found half a mile along the lane.

Walk 12

Saunderton station – Bradenham – Naphill Common – Downley
Common – Hughenden – West Wycombe – Saunderton

(11 miles)

ALTERNATIVE
Bradenham – Naphill Common – Downley Common
– Bradenham (5 miles)

OS maps 165 and 175
Sketch map 12

P Bradenham village, beside green GR 827972
Station: Saunderton BR

The 10 mile walk to Hughenden Manor from Saunderton can also
be shortened by 3 miles if you park at Bradenham. The route skirts
Naphill and goes mainly in woodland until Downley is reached,
when it turns due east to go downhill to Hughenden Manor. This
modest manor house set in rolling parkland was once the home of
Benjamin Disraeli. It is now a National Trust property crammed
with Disraeli memorabilia and with some of the rooms still as they
were when he occupied them with his wife. There is also a
National Trust shop on the site and a good tearoom. Don't forget
to check the opening times beforehand, and do visit the church
while you're about it.

From Saunderton station turn left (east) towards the A4010 and
proceed south along the wide verge of this fairly busy road for
rather more than a mile to where the Red Lion marks the
approach to Bradenham. Turn left for Bradenham village, which
you will want to explore.

This little gem is now in the care of the National Trust, and, as
always with NT properties, the care and conservation shows. The
flint and stone church was restored by the Victorians, and they
preserved the best of 700 years of history including the bells cast in

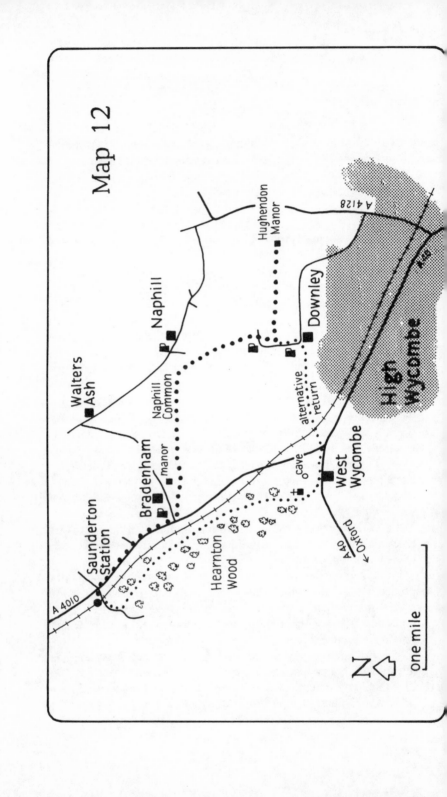

Map 12

the reign of Edward I; the Norman south doorway remains, too. Bradenham Manor, Disraeli's boyhood home, can be seen through the ornamental gateway, and if you are lucky there will be cricket on the village green.

For the route to West Wycombe, skirt the green to the right as you enter the village and take the gravelled path that goes behind the manor house. After a short distance the track splits and the narrower path to West Wycombe goes off sharp right into woodland, where instead of turning right for West Wycombe you keep to the broader track alongside the wall of the manor. When the track splits take the right-hand fork, which develops into a route going due east across Naphill Common. The Common is criss-crossed with paths so the route is sometimes obscure, but remember the route is *east*, and you will be OK. Continue for a good mile, when you will end at a broad track behind houses at Naphill. Turn right here and keep to this track for another good mile SSE to Downley Common. Again, keep to the track, and some 200 yards beyond the last house you will come to a clear bridleway crossing*. Turn left onto this bridleway for another mile due east, downhill now, first through woodland then across open land, to Hughenden.

Once again, *if you've parked at Bradenham you should return the same way*, but walkers using Saunderton station should return via West Wycombe. For this route, return from Hughenden to * above, but instead of turning right for the return to Naphill continue as you are, bearing left with the track as, quite soon, it becomes a paved path between houses. Turn left at the T-junction and cross to Downley Post Office where, on the left, a FP sign points you between houses west then south to pass in front of the school, and then goes off due west for 1½ miles on a paved way. This way eventually goes under the railway and passes a few houses to emerge almost at the junction of the A4010 and the A40. Continue west beside the A40 through West Wycombe village, returning to Saunderton on the route from St Laurence's church. Cross the hilltop from the church towards the car exit, then turn left along the lane a short distance to Windyhaugh House. Keep to this same north-westerly track as it goes in and out of Hearnton Wood for the best part of 3½ miles, ignoring all turnings off, until it comes at last to a paved lane at the foot of Slough Hill. Turn right here, and Saunderton station will be found half a mile along the lane.

4   Walks in the Chess Valley

The River Chess flows briefly from Chesham to Rickmansworth, 13 miles of clear chalk trout stream flowing for the most part through a wooded valley. Cattle graze the water meadows standing kneedeep beside the bridge where trees brush their leaves in the water, swans laze in the shallows, and the weekend walker can be there in well under the hour from Baker Street.

The Metropolitan line stations of Rickmansworth, Chorleywood, Chenies & Latimer (which, in fact, is in Little Chalfont and near neither of the two villages for which it is named) and Chesham are the four which serve the area; Amersham, Great Missenden and Wendover, the other three stations on the line, are mentioned in another chapter. The branch line to Chesham is threatened constantly with axing and the station with closure, but each time the subject comes up the residents protest vigorously and once more the line is reprieved.

There are walks of great number and variety from these four stations, of which a few are suggested in this chapter, but for a general introduction to the Chess Valley you could hardly do better than this walk along the River Chess, an easy, level route with much of interest along the way.

Walk 13

**Chesham station – Chesham Moor – Blackwell Hall Lane – Latimer
– Latimer Bottom – Chenies – Mount Wood – Sarratt Bottom –
Little Lady's Wood – Rickmansworth**

(12 miles)

ALTERNATIVES
Return to Chesham from Blackwell Hall Lane
(6 miles)
Return to Chorleywood station from Chenies
(10 miles)

OS maps 165 and 176
Sketch map 13

P Public carparks behind Chesham High Street
Station: Chesham (Met. Line from Baker St)

The source of the river is said to be Skottowes Pond, in Lowndes
Park, where an eighteenth-century developer probably made use
of the natural spring to provide himself with an ornamental water.
So from Chesham station turn left for the High Street, crossing
over to take the first on the left behind the War Memorial. This
short road will bring you to Lowndes Park. Follow the lakeside
through the park until the spire of St Mary's church comes into
view, and make across the green towards it. You will find a
pathway that will bring you out into Church Street.

Turn right and continue along Church Street with its interesting
variety of buildings until you come to the Queen's Head, where
you will get your first sight of the river proper. Follow the river
round left on the narrow path. In wet seasons it goes a bit wild
here and floods everywhere – over the path, into the gardens,
under the sheds on the right and wherever else it can get – but it is
soon tamed and runs sedately, all weeds and watercress, to Water
Lane, where it crosses under Germain Street at the Town Bridge.

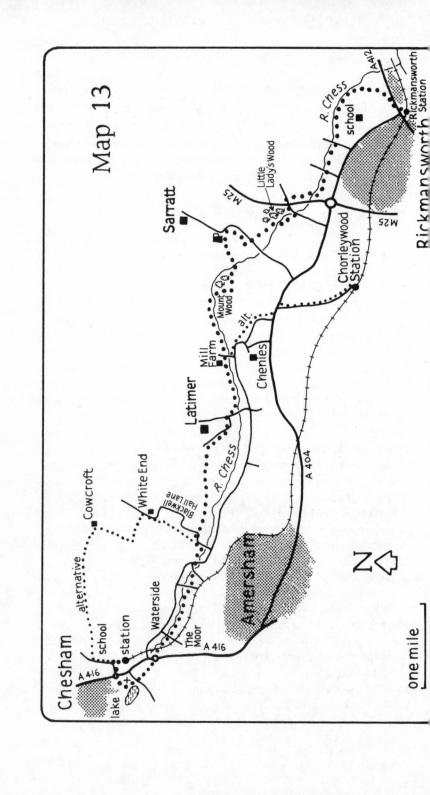

Map 13

Leave the river where it enters Germain Street, and turn right to cross over and take the asphalt path beside Thomas Harding School (named after Thomas Harding, the Chesham martyr, burned for his faith under Bloody Mary). This narrow way passes some nice examples of brick and flint, the Buckinghamshire vernacular, before emerging into Amy Lane where you proceed to the small roundabout and take the road opposite to pick up the river again beside offices and follow it onto Chesham Moor.

Ignore the iron footbridge on the left when you come to it, keeping instead across the front of the houses ahead to cross Bois Moor Road and return to the moor via a passageway and a narrow bridge. Now you can follow the riverside path very pleasantly for the best part of a mile, enjoying the ducks and coots and wagtails and the gardens on the far bank, until the footpath ends and brings you back to the road. Here you have a choice: you can follow the road for half a mile, or you can take the footpath on your right signposted Lower Bois. Neither route is ideal. The first traverses a busy road where there is no real provision for pedestrians; the second starts out as a muddy, enclosed path past the sewage works. Of the two I marginally prefer the latter, which definitely improves after a while, and if you decide upon it turn left after the kissing gate and keep round to the edge of the field to a stile beside an iron gate, proceeding up that path to Holloway Lane where you will meet the river again.

Turn right into Latimer Road at the top of Holloway Lane, where you will meet up with your friends who have taken the other route. In either case, your destination is Blackwell Hall Lane, which leaves Latimer Road opposite Ivy House Farm, 500 yards south-east of the Thames Water Authority's ground in Latimer Road.

Once you turn into this quiet lane you are in another world. The waterfall below the bridge, the enclosing trees and the old, brooding houses show England at its best, and you will want to linger here. Unfortunately the same warning applies: this is a narrow lane without footpaths, and busy. So continue up the lane to Blackwell Farm on the right; your path lies ahead here while the paved lane goes off left.

The map shows a let-out here for those wishing to return to Chesham station, which, if followed, will give you a round walk of some 6 miles in all. Instead of taking the Latimer footpath, turn left with the lane for half a mile to a left-hand fork, where another paved lane leads to White End. On reaching the white house on the left along this lane, ignore the footpath before the house and carry on instead to another FP 100 yards on. This FP and bridleway runs north-west for a short mile through Cowcroft Wood to Cowcroft Farm and hamlet. Just past the hamlet, the same bridleway turns sharply left (west) to continue another 1½ miles in a NNW loop above Dungrove Farm, before coming back due west to the railway, which it follows back to Chesham station.

Our principal route lies along the unmade farm road off Blackwell Hall Lane, to the left of Blackwell Farm and to the right of the new house set back from green lawns. When the path splits keep to the right of the field hedge. Look back as you go: the studding on the back wall of Blackwell Farm is not to be missed.

This footpath continues within sight of the road and the river for roughly a third of a mile, until the river takes a loop north-easterly, when the path also goes ENE another half mile to skirt Frith Wood and emerge onto the road beside Parkfield Latimer, a private estate which formerly belonged to the National Defence College, and is so marked on OS maps. Turn right (south) on this pretty lane where the far crest is crowned with all the greens of mixed woodland, and follow it to Latimer village, a placid joy of old, dark-brick cottages scattered around a tiny green.

At the junction with the main road through Latimer village turn right again, where, after a few yards, a FP goes off left (east), following the river again through Latimer Bottom until it comes back to the road again at Mill Farm (eggs and cream for sale). To visit Chenies village, continue up the lane past Mill Farm and Dodds Mill, turning left as you come to the road ahead when a few hundred yards will bring you to Chenies. The church and manor here are very fine, and the manor is open to the public Wednesday and Thursday afternoon 2 till 5 from April to October, Bank Holiday Mondays 2 till 6, and serving teas. There are also two good pubs for refreshment.

There is another escape route from Chenies, for those who have had enough, reducing the walk to no more than 10 miles. For this, continue through Chenies village to the main A404, which you cross to walk left (east) along the verge until you come to Green Street on the right, with Great Greenstreet Farm on one corner and Little

Greenstreet Farm on the other. A mile away at the far end of Green Street is Chorleywood station, where you can return to your starting place, be it the main line station or a carpark in Chesham.

After visiting Chenies, turn left up the paved lane past Mill Farm to a FP signposted right which goes first through water meadows, then through a copse, then back towards the river bank to a bridge over the river at Valley Farm. Cross here, taking the FP immediately on the right which goes east then south through Mount Wood. Here you can see through the trees and across the watercress beds to the river below in the valley, while all around in springtime are bluebells and other woodland flowers and in autumn russet leaves and beechmast. Enjoy this half mile of bliss before the next footbridge takes you back across the river to Sarratt Bottom, to turn right again onto a crossing footpath (watch out for this) to come to the road again at Sarratt.

Sarratt village, with its pubs, pond and long village green, lies half a mile left along this road, but only 100 yards away in the same direction is The Cock offering bar snacks.

From the church opposite the pub, cross the road to the signposted footpath by Goldingtons, which crosses fields in a south-west/south-east/south-west dogleg, crossing one paved road on the way, back to the river again.

Here you are in part of the Chorleywood House estate, a public open space, and for half a mile you have the freedom of the river bank: a favourite picnic place, especially in school holidays. The way forward, past the white-painted riverside house away on the left, brings you to a paved path which will take you, via a kissing gate, to Solesbridge Lane: another of those narrow lanes with no provision for pedestrians.

A short distance along here to the left the path takes a diversion to accommodate the M25, so follow Solesbridge Lane over the motorway then cross to where the footpath dives down right beside the Highland Water Gardens, for a nasty 300 yards or so due south, fenced off from the fast road. Soon the route turns south-east again across farmlands to skirt Little Lady's Wood and come within half a mile to the houses of Loudwater private estate. The FP is carefully signposted between the houses and back to fields again, and after a quarter of a mile or so emerges onto the roadway at Loudwater Lane. Turn left up the lane for a few yards where another FP opposite goes for a while between fences before coming back to the river again.

You have come a good way now, but take heart, there is only a long mile left to Rickmansworth station and the end of the journey, and one of the most pleasant miles of the day. Soon you will come to a footbridge, but keep to the near bank and you will find yourself following the river beside well-kept greensward, so kindly to tired feet. Even when the path says goodbye to the Chess for the last time to bend west and pass between school playing-fields, it is still pleasant and leafy. It continues so to the last, coming eventually to an end beside a public open space by Rickmansworth Park Primary School.

Here bear right by the school carpark to climb a mound and strike diagonally left to the top left-hand corner of the green, where you cross the bridge ahead and descend the steps for Rickmansworth station.

The next two walks give an opportunity to walk beside the Chess without following the whole length of the river. These are circular walks from Chorleywood or Rickmansworth stations, and since these stations are little more than half an hour from Baker Street or Marylebone this is a good area for walking on the long evenings of summer.

Walk 14

Chorleywood station – Chorleywood House – Sarratt – Chenies – Chorleywood

(6 miles)

ALTERNATIVES
From Sarratt to Chenies via three farms
(5 miles)
From Sarratt to Chenies with diversion to Chipperfield Common
(5 miles)

OS map 166
Sketch map 14

P Public carpark on Chorleywood Common GR 028961
Station: Chorleywood (Met. line from Baker St.)

From the main entrance at Chorleywood station turn left to the bottom of the hill and cross to take the private road going steeply up on the right to Chorleywood Common. At the top of this hill (Colleyland), cross and turn left again to keep around the edge of the common, north and north-east and for half a mile to the A404 Amersham–Rickmansworth road. Here cross again to enter the gates of Chorleywood House, opposite.

Chorleywood House estate is a public open space in the care of Three Rivers District Council. The house was built in 1895 by Lady Ela Russell, sister of the then Duke of Bedford, to her own design and for her own occupation at a time when the Russell family still owned great chunks of the Chess Valley. The family crest and motto 'Che sera sera' ('What will be will be') can still be seen on the east wall of the house.

Pass across the front of the house, then, and go round the side and bear a little right beneath the great trees towards an iron gate ahead giving onto a paved path; turn right. Unbelievably, prisoners of war were kept behind the wire mesh of the compound

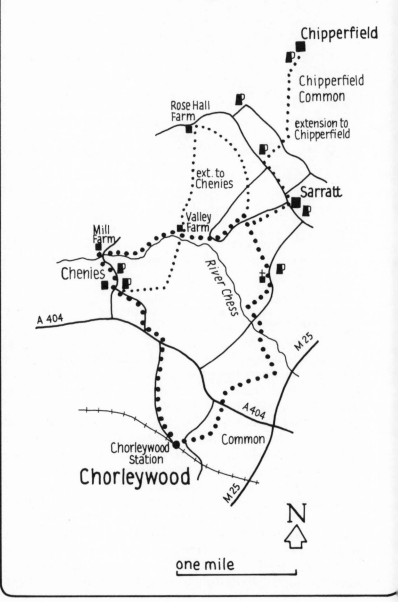

Map 14

Chipperfield

Chipperfield
Common

extension to
Chipperfield

Rose Hall
Farm

ext. to
Chenies

Sarratt

Mill
Farm

Valley
Farm

River Chess

Chenies

A 404

M 25

A 404

Chorleywood
Station

Common

Chorleywood

M 25

N

one mile

on the left here during the Second World War, housed in the green-painted wooden huts where the Chorleywood Players now store their scenery.

Follow the paved path east then north-east as it becomes ever rougher and narrower to wind down through a rough copse to the water meadows of the River Chess, which here is a shallow chalk stream running between green banks, with a wooden bridge crossing.

Cross the bridge (NB the bridge on the left; not the bridge to the private house on the right) and take the path beyond, which crosses fields in a dog leg bearing NNE/NNW/NW, crossing one small road on the way, to emerge opposite Sarratt church. This was the original settlement – church, manor house and pub (The Cock, 50 yards along the road to the right), but Sarratt village is now settled around a long village green the best part of a mile to the north. Note the church, which has the only saddleback tower in Hertfordshire.

Take the right-hand FP behind the church due north for half a mile and, ignoring the crossing path halfway, emerge beside a nursery in Dawes Lane. Sarratt village, duckpond, pubs and village green are right, at the top of this lane.

A pleasant 2 miles can be added to this short walk by taking the dotted diversion shown in the sketch map. This starts from the nursery in Dawes Lane, where the church path continues across the lane and runs due north across farm land, skirting the edge of Rosehall Wood then making north-west to Rose Hall Farm. The path passes to the nearside of the farm, then takes a sharp left-hand to return south another mile to the ford over the Chess at Valley Farm. Then, as an alternative to the return to Chenies village across the watermeadows described in the main route below, you could cross the ford to the south bank of the river, taking a FP immediately up on your left steeply south through Mount Wood to Mount Wood Farm, where the path bears due west to end behind the Red Lion in Chenies village. This is a good alternative when the watermeadows are too muddy.

Another diversion could take you from Sarratt village green to a FP on the right just past the Boot which runs ENE across fields to cross Plough Lane, then on two-thirds of a mile north-west and north to Chipperfield Common, a favourite spot, with the Two Brewers Inn and cricket on the green. Return to Sarratt and continue on either the route above or the principal route below.

Turn left along Dawes Lane to the end, then sharp left again onto the FP which goes west along the river, though not continuously beside it, another mile to the road bridge at Mill Farm. This riverside path can be very mucky in wet weather. Continue up the road past Mill Farm to cross the Chess by Dodds Mill, turning left again at the T-junction for Chenies village. Care is needed on the busy, narrow road here, but a FP running high above the road on the right will allow you to walk safely for part of the way. Roe deer are sometimes seen here.

Chenies church and manor lie along the gravel path to the right as you enter the village. Chenies church is described by Pevsner as 'The richest storehouse of funeral monuments in any parish church in England'; it is a delightful little church in flint with stone dressings set in a beautifully kept churchyard. The hammerbeam roof is Victorian, but apart from the Bedford monuments there are some good brasses and a Norman font. The manor is open from April to October, Wednesdays, Thursdays and spring and summer bank holidays, 2pm to 5pm. It has lovely gardens, including a physic garden, and serves good teas.

Continue on through the village (two pubs – the Bedford Arms [posh] and the Red Lion [plebeian]) to the A404; cross the road and turn left along the verge a short distance, then turn right at Green Street, where Great Greenstreet Farm is on one corner and Little Greenstreet Farm on the other, and after a scant mile along the verge here you will come to houses and to Chorleywood station. In autumn you can fill your sandwich bag along here with enough blackberries for a good pie.

Walk 15

Rickmansworth station – Croxley Moor – Batchworth lock – Harefield – Maple Cross – Ladywalk Wood – Chorleywood – Loudwater – River Chess – Rickmansworth

(15 miles)

ALTERNATIVES
End at Chorleywood
(10½ miles)
Return to Rickmansworth from Batchworth lock
(3 miles)

OS map
Sketch map 15

P Public carpark off Rickmansworth High Street GR 058946
Station: Rickmansworth (Met. line from Baker St.)

The next walk starts from Rickmansworth station and goes along the canal to Harefield, then to Chorleywood and back via the Chess to Rickmansworth.

Turn right from the station and walk up Station Road to turn left and cross over to walk the length of Rickmansworth High Street. Soon after passing the St Joan of Arc School, a FP sign points right between office blocks to 'Croxley Moor & Canal'. This straight path runs for half a mile due east between the railway line on the left and extensive school playing-fields on the right, giving a last view of the River Chess at the start. Where the path forks at Croxley Farm, take the left fork for 200 yards or so to come to the canal beside a lock cottage, and turn right along the towpath for a good half mile walk to Batchworth lock.

This is one of the few stretches of the canal with permanent or semi-permanent moorings, and among the boats which are almost head to tail here you will find fine examples of canal narrow boats painted with the traditional Roses & Castles designs. It makes a

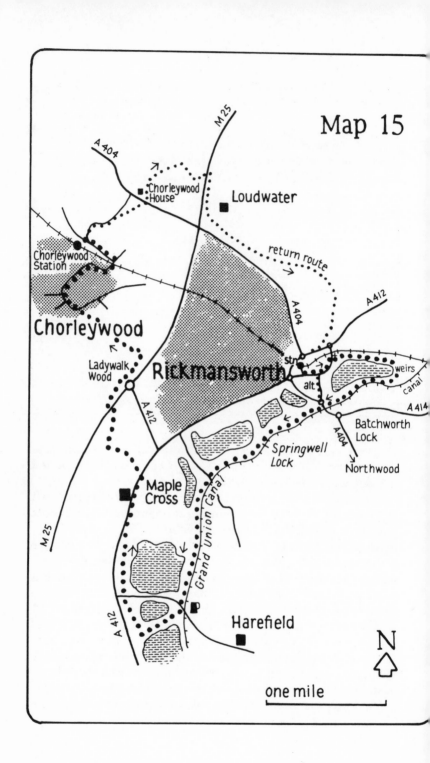

Map 15

good walk for children: not too long and with plenty of interest. *At Batchworth lock you could leave the canal and turn right to walk up to the roundabout and on along Church Street to return to Rickmansworth High Street and station, giving a short walk of some 3 miles.*

To continue to Harefield, keep to the towpath and soon you will be passing Rickmansworth Aquadrome (to which there is access via a wooden bridge) on the right. The route then proceeds for 2 interesting miles along the towpath passing Stockers lock and Springwell lock to reach the Fisheries Inn beside the broad reaches of Coppermill Lock at Harefield. The route leaves the canal here, to take the FP signposted across the Fisheries carpark. This FP soon crosses a factory road at a stile to go through a gap in the far hedge by the notice board of a private angling club. Then it continues due west across a narrow isthmus, at places a mere 6 feet wide, between two great lakes formed by gravel extraction. Fishermen's lakes they are now, where enthusiasts sit out the night in the season with rods and sleeping bags and thermos flasks, waiting for the dawn.

After an all too brief quarter mile the path emerges onto the Old Uxbridge Road, now a quiet backwater superseded by the A412, which has itself been superseded by the M25. Here you will turn right for about 800 yards until your path joins the main road. Keep to the broad verge here until you can cross at the traffic lights at Maple Cross, and on the far side of the road, at the foot of a pedestrian bridge, a private road and a bridlepath go off left to Woodoaks Farm. Make up here towards the farm buildings ahead, bearing right past the farmhouse to the last opening in the old brick wall, which gives onto the bridleway.

Behind you is the hustle of the A412 and a rash of blue motorway signs, but here all is peace as you go uphill between fields to where the trees of Ladywalk Wood crown the ridge. (It is called 'Ladywalk' because it is haunted by the ghost of a lady in riding habit, though there is no sign of the horse.) Follow the FP keeping to the right through the trees until you can turn left onto the long footbridge that carries the path high over the M25, turning right again on the far side to follow the paved path down to the road to Heronsgate. Cross this road with care to where the FP continues opposite, briefly beside the motorway, before bearing off left across fields for the best part of a mile to Chorleywood.

Halfway along another path goes off right; ignore it, and keep to the bridleway which will bring you in due course out through a farmyard onto a narrow lane.

This is Stag Lane, Chorleywood. Turn left here for a short distance to pass the school, and take the first immediate right. Make downhill between houses, turning right again at the bottom and following this road (Chorleywood Bottom) past the pub and green on your left and over the narrow railway bridge, to turn sharp left for Chorleywood station. *You could end your walk here and take the train, giving a walk from Rickmansworth of 10½ miles, which for interest and variety takes a lot of beating. The walk beside the railway across Croxley Moor, the canal boats and locks, the cows and cornfields and creeper-clad farmhouse, and finally the eerie sense of detachment as you cross the motorway high above the whizzing traffic, all make for a memorable day out, with plenty of places for refreshment along the way.*

Should you wish to walk back to Rickmansworth instead of taking the train from Chorleywood station, proceed as follows. From the main entrance at Chorleywood station turn left to the bottom of the hill and cross to take the private road going steeply up on the right to Chorleywood Common. At the top of this hill (Colleyland), cross and turn left again to keep around the edge of the common, north and north-east for half a mile to the A404 Amersham–Rickmansworth road. Here cross again to enter the gates of Chorleywood House, opposite.

Pass across the front of the house, then, and go round the side and bear a little right beneath the great trees towards an iron gate ahead giving onto a paved path; turn right.

Follow the paved path east then north-east as it becomes ever rougher and narrower to wind down through a rough copse to the water meadows of the River Chess, which here is a shallow chalk stream running between green banks, with a wooden bridge crossing. Then without crossing the river turn back south-east (right) and follow the paved path ahead to arrive via a gate onto a narrow leafy lane between houses.

Now the FP is diverted to cross the M25, so turn left along the lane until you have crossed the motorway, when you will see a FP sign right beside the Highland Water Gardens. This FP takes you for a short boring distance beside the motorway before emerging to cross fields, go briefly through a wood, and cross more fields to emerge between houses at Loudwater. The route is carefully signposted here between the houses; remember your route is south-easterly.

Skirting the backs of the houses, the route then goes beside another wood before crossing a narrow road to recommence on the far side between fences. Soon you will be back to the river again, now flowing swift and clear under a broad grassy bank. After 1½ miles of this most agreeable path, which all too soon leaves the river behind, and you will have arrived at Rickmansworth.

The path comes out to a church and primary school. Pass across the front of the school to go over the grassy mound ahead and make for the far left-hand corner of the playing-field, where you will cross the footbridge and descend to Rickmansworth station.

At nearly 15 miles this is a long walk, but it is undemanding and full of interest, and there is a let-out at Chorleywood if you are weary.

Walk 16

Chorleywood station – Shire Lane – Chilterns Open Air Museum – Chalfont St Giles – Chorleywood

(7½ miles)

ALTERNATIVES
From Chalfont St Giles – Jordans – Seer Green
(10½ miles)
From Chalfont St Giles – Jordans – Chorleywood
(12 miles)
From Chalfont St Giles – Jordans – Goldhill Common – Chalfont
St Peter – Chalfont St Giles – Chorleywood
(15 miles)

OS maps 175 and 176
Sketch map 16

P Public carpark on Chorleywood Common GR 028961
Station: Chorleywood (Met. line from Baker St.)

Chorleywood station is the starting point for many good walks, apart from those centred on the River Chess. This next walk through beech woods gives the chance to visit the Chilterns Open Air Museum, Milton's Cottage and the Quaker Meeting House at Chalfont St Giles, and Chalfont St Peter if wished.

Leave Chorleywood station by the main entrance to walk downhill and turn left under the bridge. You are now in Shire Lane, which separates Hertfordshire from Buckinghamshire. Our route follows Shire Lane for the best part of 2 miles. For the first half mile it is a leafy avenue divided by a narrow island of woodland, then the avenue bears off left to become Heronsgate Road and we continue straight on along Old Shire Lane, with fields on the right. Here in the hedge blackthorn, hawthorn, dog rose, honeysuckle and blackberry bloom in fine progression through the seasons, sheltering at their feet celandines, stitchwort

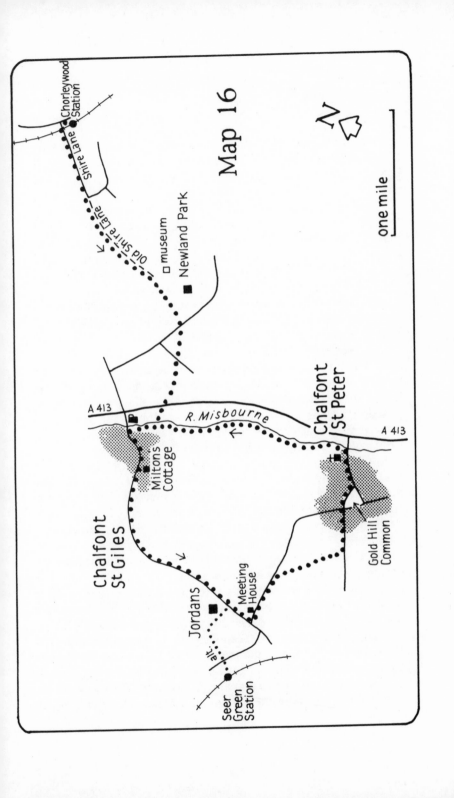

Map 16

N

one mile

Chorleywood Station

Shire Lane

Old Shire Lane

museum
Newland Park

A 413

R. Misbourne

Chalfont St Peter

A 413

Miltons Cottage

Chalfont St Giles

Gold Hill Common

Jordans

Meeting House

alt.

Seer Green Station

and campion. Ahead you can see the massy, tall beeches of Phillipshill Wood.

Keep going due south-west, ignoring all gates, stiles or turnings off until you come to a five-barred gate on the right where the bridleway (as the lane has by now become) turns sharp left. Through the trees here you can see a square water tower and one of the buildings of the Chilterns Open Air Museum. There is no access to the Museum at this point, though.

Climb the stile on your right and follow the obvious path, still bearing south-west by fields and woods, to emerge after a short mile onto the tarmac path beside the lodge gates of Newland Park, currently a Bucks. County College of Further Education. To visit the Open Air Museum (open Sundays and Bank Holidays 2–5.30pm), you will turn left along the tarmac path.

This museum is a Chiltern Society project; among other items rebuilt here are a medieval cruck-framed barn from Berkshire, the High Wycombe Toll House, a cart-shed brought from Didcot, a granary saved from a farm near Berkhamsted and another of the same from Wing, and a representation of an Iron Age hut. In addition there is a nature trail on the north-facing chalk slope. The leaflet tells you to expect a variety of chalk grassland flora, including cowslips and wood sorrel, and a great variety of butterflies – brimstone, meadow-brown, gatekeeper, small heath, tortoiseshell, and the rarer speckled wood.

After visiting the museum, return to the path and go out through the lodge gates to cross the road and take the track into the woods opposite on a bearing WSW. After 500 yards or so you cross another lane and continue, with the path now going more westerly, to pass through a group of pleasant houses and emerge onto the road at the Pheasant crossroads on the approach to Chalfont St Giles village. Pheasant Hill, going steeply down beside the inn, will bring you to the village green.

There are several good pubs here, one with a garden; a duck pond, a church with remains of fourteenth-century wall paintings and a peaceful churchyard; and 300 yards along the road, Milton's cottage, open 1st March to 30th October, Tuesdays to Saturdays 10am–1pm and 2–6pm. Milton came to St Giles from London in 1665 to escape the Plague, having written to his friend Thomas Ellwood to request that he find a suitable house. Already blind, he missed the hustle of the city and returned there as soon as the Great

Fire had swept it clean, but while at his 'pretty box', as he called the cottage, he finished *Paradise Lost* and started on the sequel.

The cottage was bought by public subscription in 1887 to commemorate queen Victoria's Jubilee, the Queen herself heading the list with a donation of £20. It was refurbished in 1977 for the Jubilee of our present Queen. There is a roomful of Milton memorabilia, and the museum is very popular with the Americans who come to see the grave of William Penn in the Quaker burial ground at Jordans. Our main route now returns to Chorleywood by this same route, giving a walk of 7½ miles. For those wishing to extend their walk two alternatives are given below.

One option is to Seer Green station, returning to London on the Princes Risborough line to Marylebone. But please remember that at no point, except at Marylebone, does this connect with the Metropolitan line. Another word of caution: this walk to Jordans is mainly along a narrow lane where for much of the way there is no verge; it might be wiser, therefore, not to attempt it when walking with large parties or with children.

Keep to the main road through St Giles from Milton's cottage, ignoring all roads off, until you have passed right through the village and come to a lane on the left signposted 'Jordans'. You will come to the historic Quaker Meeting House, Guesthouse and Mayflower Barn two-thirds of a mile along this lane.

The simple Meeting House (second oldest in England) was built in 1688, and in the quiet burial ground are the graves of many famous Quakers: William Penn and his two wives, Thomas Ellwood, Isaac and Mary Pennington, and Joseph Rule, known as The White Quaker from his habit of making his clothes of undyed cloth. The same plain headstones mark the graves of all who are buried here. But if you are not interested in history or headstones, come in spring to see the massed daffodils or at any time of year for a plain tea served at the plain, scrubbed tables of the Guest House.

The road to Jordans village is almost opposite the entrance to the Guest House; for Seer Green station, keep straight on through Jordans village with the playing-field on your right, to the first crossroads, where turn left and follow the path as it loops to the right to emerge opposite Farm Road, which leads up to the station.

Jordans village was founded by the Quaker community in 1919 with the object of 'building up a society of men and women who make no distinction between different forms of labour'. The houses around the green were built by and for working men, professional men and artist/craftsmen (and for 'men' read also 'women'), not all of them Quakers. An account of the building of Jordans village and the changes that came about over the years can be found in the book Jordans, the Making of a Community, *by A.L. Hayward, of which copies are available at the Guesthouse.*

From the Quaker Meeting House there is a route to Chalfont St Peter, for those with time and stamina, or perhaps a route to be enjoyed separately on another occasion.

Turn left (east) from the Meeting House up Welders Lane for some 300 yards to a FP on the right going roughly two-thirds of a mile south-east, partly through woods, and emerging onto the road at Layters Green near the pond, when Chalfont St Peter is clearly to be seen to the left.

Making towards St Peter, you will come to Goldhill Common, a large high green with children's swings and roundabouts. Keep around the left-hand (north) side of the common to come downhill into the village proper. This is the old village street of Chalfont St Peter, and ends at the church and the Greyhound Inn. Here you will catch a glimpse of the River Misbourne, flowing between banks bright and pungent in spring with garlicky white ramsons. The river appears briefly here, but if you follow the FP signposted NNE past the playing-fields and allotments you will find it again, and will be able to follow it back for best part of 2 miles to Chalfont St Giles. This diversion is of interest, as it shows the considerable difference between the carefully preserved village of Chalfont St Giles and the much more towny sister village, once every bit as pretty but now a world away with an ugly roundabout, bypass and new shopping precinct.

Walk 17

Chesham station – Little Hundridge Lane – Herbert's Hole Cottage
– Ballinger Bottom – The Lee – King's Ash – Wendover

(9½ miles)

ALTERNATIVES
Return to Great Missenden from Herbert's Hole Cottage via
South Heath and Frith Hill
(5 miles)
Diversion to Pednor House and Little Pednor

OS map 165
Sketch map 17

P Public carparks to west of Chesham High Street GR 958018
Station: Chesham (Met. line from Baker St.)

There is some argument for including this next walk, which runs towards Great Missenden and Wendover, in the Misbourne Valley chapter, but a glance at the map indicates otherwise. The dry valleys, and hence also the lanes and footpaths, all centre on Chesham, making the obvious choice to bring them in here.

Some of the lanes that follow the valleys westwards from Chesham are hollow ways lined with trees or topped with old, deep hedges, and one has but to study the map to understand their origin in the footfalls that marked them out over the centuries from outlying settlements to marketplace and town: Hundridge Manor and Little Hundridge Farm, Pednor House and Farms, Hawthorne Farm, Bassibones Farm, Hunts Green Farm – all lie along or at the end of narrow country lanes and pathways centred on the ancient town.

The same pattern can be traced to north and east, for Chesham is one of the oldest towns in Buckinghamshire, with a Royal Grant of a three-day fair in 1257 and a parish church with a great lump of Hertfordshire puddingstone in its foundations begun a century earlier.

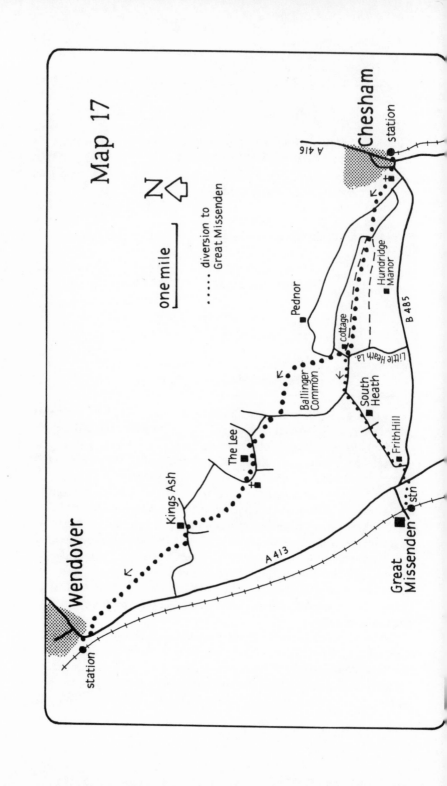

Map 17

Chesham old town is centred on Church Street and Germain Street. Cheek by jowl here stand early and late Georgian, early and late Victorian and some Edwardian buildings, plus a terrace of Queen Anne houses with white shutters, and a courtyard of flint-faced cottages with their backs to Lowndes Park. A pair of dwellings at 54 Church Street, built in the fourteenth-century, still has the original king post and trusses which supported the first roof, as a plaque on the front of the house tells us, and the grand house at The Bury which is now in use as solicitors' offices was built in 1712 to the order of Sir William Lowndes, Secretary to the Treasury for Queen Anne. 'Mr. Secretary Ways & Means' he was called, from his constantly saying 'Take care of the pence and the pounds will take care of themselves'. We cannot argue that his did.

No. 86 Church Street is a good example of chequered brickwork using Chesham Blues, the vitrified bricks produced by the local custom of firing bricks on the updraught, causing a glazing of some bricks by steam. These blue bricks are really the failures, but they were kept for ornamentation and sometimes used as headers in a chequered pattern, as here, or to pick out a date or a set of initials. This use is common in south Bucks, and it is interesting to look out for it along the way.

From Chesham station turn left up to the High Street, turning right towards the war memorial then left past the Baptist Church and carparks to enter Lowndes Park, which you will see ahead beyond the far roundabout. Don't miss the Gatehouse development opposite the Baptist church; now an estate agent's office, this is a craftsman-restored medieval survival the like of which it is rarely one's privilege to see. For an account of the fascinating details involved in this building's chance discovery and restoration, see the author's *Picture of Buckinghamshire*, (Robert Hale, 1983.)

On reaching the lake, Skottowe's Pond, to give it a name, you have a choice to continue on the main route or *to take half an hour to explore the old town: if the latter is your plan, follow the path around the lake, making towards the church which soon comes into sight ahead. You will come out into Church Street between St Mary's church and The Bury. ('Bury', incidentally, is no more than the Hertfordshire word for 'Place'.)*

Walkers caught up in an exploration of the old town and finding themselves where the infant Chess bubbles up from its culvert opposite the junction of roads to Pednormead End and Missenden might notice that the OS map offers an alternative route here to Little Hundridge Lane, starting from Misbourne Road, at the entrance to Lower Hundridge Farm and passing close to Great Hundridge Manor. Though it would save retracing steps back to the main route across Lowndes Park, this route involves half a mile at the start along the verge of a fast road, and the footpath itself, when reached, is narrow and little-used. Also, it gives no view of the manor, passing to the back of it with a thick hedge between. Best to return, therefore, to the park and rejoin the original route.

The main route leaves Skottowe's Pond in a north-westerly direction, with the pond at your back and the children's swings on your left. You should make for a pair of stiles in the top left-hand corner.

From these stiles the route descends to cross the Pednor road and take the left one of two paths crossing the field opposite, which brings you in turn to Drydell Lane.

Turn right onto this paved lane where you will quickly come to a small triangle of parking space at the start of a bridlepath. *This path is one of three routes from here to Little Hundridge Lane, but not the best, being enclosed for the most part between high hedges and invariably muddy.* Ignore it, and go instead through the farm gate just around the corner, where a good unmarked footpath goes west across the rolling farming country of Hundridge Farm Estate. There are lambs in the meadows in early spring, and later the land is golden with oilseed rape, its pungent scent all around. After a very pleasant 1½ miles, Little Hundridge Lane is reached at a three-way junction by Herbert's Hole Cottage.

There is a third route to this road junction at Herbert's Hole which is useful when the footpaths are very muddy. At Drydell Lane, instead of taking the farm path described above, follow the lane on past the farm gate, as it goes first north then west. It is a pleasant, little-used lane lined with bright hedges, and towards the end it takes you past Pednor House, an Elizabethan timber-framed building with an eighteenth-century façade. A little further on the lane goes through Little Pednor, which Pevsner describes as 'A remarkably successful enlargement of some farm buildings to make a formal composition round an oblong courtyard, through which runs the main road'. If you want to walk the farm path and see Pednor, turn right along the lane at Herbert's Hole Cottage and walk north about 500 yards when you will come to a junction with Drydell Lane; turn right there, and Little Pednor will be found in 100 yards or so.

At the three-way junction by Herbert's Hole Cottage the decision must be taken whether to press on to Wendover or go down to Great Missenden, which is under 2 miles or so away. Gluttons for punishment could do both, having a quick pie and a pint in one of Missenden's many good pubs before returning to this junction to continue the walk. This would add a good 3 miles, over all, to the journey.

For the shorter route to Great Missenden, then, take the road due west from Herbert's Hole Cottage, the centre one of the three, bearing left at the next junction to go through South Heath on a south-westerly route, keeping to the road until it joins a slightly larger road, Frith Hill. Cross Frith Hill and take the footpath opposite which leads you past the handsome church of St Peter and Paul to a bridge across the main road and so into Great Missenden.

For Wendover, turn very briefly left at Herbert's Hole Cottage to take the FP immediately right; keep to this northerly footpath, ignoring all forks or paths off, for a good half mile until it bends to the left to emerge onto the road at Ballinger Bottom. Cross here to take up the FP again on the far side of the road for a pleasant mile north-west across Lee Common, coming into the picture village of The Lee at Hawthorne Farm. There are two pubs here: one almost opposite you and another, the Cock & Rabbit, round the corner to your right at the far side of the village.

The route on to King's Ash leaves The Lee from behind Church Farm, at the west end of the village by the Church of St John the Baptist. Go up the farm road, and at the end of a brief paved section the way forks, the left-hand path going west to King's Lane and the one on the right a mile across fields to King's Ash Farm. Take the right-hand path, and when you emerge onto the lane at King's Ash turn left for 100 yards to Hogtrough Lane on the right. This is an old green road, at times a typical hollow way, which takes you all the way to Wendover. After half a mile the Ridgeway LDFP comes in from the right; follow the Ridgeway signs onwards from the church on the approach to Wendover, and they will take you along Wendover High Street to the Metropolitan line station.

(NB To return by train from Great Missenden or Wendover to Chesham involves going right back along the line to Chalfont &

Latimer station for the Chesham branch line, so if you are using a car and want to do the long walk to Wendover you might consider parking at Old Amersham (GR 962973), when you can walk through Shardeloes Park and Little Missenden as described in the walk along the Misbourne, Walk no. 21.)

5   Walks in the Misbourne Valley

These walks are very different in character from those in the previous chapter. Whereas the Chess Valley walks are mostly enclosed and intimate, going in short stretches from wood to water to village and again to water and wood, the walks in the valley of the Misbourne are more often over open farming country. Lush rolling fields, with occasional patches of bare chalk showing between the yellow rape seed or rippling corn, separate the villages, and though, mercifully, the Chilterns has largely escaped the mid-twentieth-century curse of prairie farming, it is more often the occasional snatch of woodland that breaks up the arable than the traditional hedge.

The Misbourne Valley is justly famous for its scenery, but the river itself is a poor thing today, dry in parts and in others no more than a trickle, and nowhere approaching the 'large stream of water 30 ft wide' reported by the Rector of Hampden as an exceptional occurrence in his parish register of 1774. The Misbourne had a reputation for quirkiness even then; accounts in old books frequently tell of the river running dry in wet winters or flooding in times of drought, the belief being that this was due as much to the action of the wind as to the clemency of the season.

A book issued by the Chiltern Society in 1987, *To Rescue a River*, by Vic Wotton, ascribes the present poor state of the Misbourne to over-abstraction by the Thames Water Authority, and the Chiltern Society has made such a fuss about this that the TWA and other responsible bodies are now trying to correct it. Chiltern Society members have done a great deal of work on the river themselves; they have restored the pond where the river rises to the north of Great Missenden, opposite the Black Horse at Mobwell, and have tried to clear the river's course between there and Deep Mill. Alas, much of the river is still dry.

Between Mobwell and Little Missenden the river runs partly over private land, as it does between Chalfont St Peter and the confluence of the Misbourne with the River Colne at Denham, and as there is no satisfactory run of footpaths close to these sections it is suggested that those who would like to walk the river bank start either at Little Missenden village or from Amersham, finishing by the church and the Greyhound Inn at Chalfont St Peter. This will cut out some road walking between Great Missenden and Grange Farm.

Walk 18

**Great Missenden station – Little Missenden – Shardeloes Park –
Amersham – Chalfont St Giles – Chalfont St Peter – Gerrards Cross**

(12 miles)

ALTERNATIVES
Start at Little Missenden
(6 miles to St Giles, 8 to St Peter)
Start at Amersham
(4 miles to St Giles, 6 to St Peter)

OS maps 165 and 175
Sketch map 18

P Link Road carpark, Great Missenden GR 894014
Past church in Little Missenden GR 921990
Behind bus station in old Amersham GR 962973
Station: Great Missenden (Met. line from Marylebone)

Leave Great Missenden station or carpark and walk SSE through
the village, continuing along the same road when the shops are left
behind until you reach the Nags Head inn, approximately a mile
away. This road roughly follows the course of the Misbourne; were
there sufficient flow the river would be seen in the fields to your
left.

Turn right past the Nags Head and left under the railway bridge
for half a mile along the road to a footpath by Grange Farm, where
you leave the road and go left again, due east, for a mile or so to
come to Little Missenden.

You could find yourself spending quite a lot of time in Little
Missenden, where there is a Jacobean Manor House and a
part-twelfth-century church in flint and clunch, as well as two good
pubs. Fortunately our route takes us right through the village, so
keep along the main road, where eventually you will find the river
running behind houses on your left, until you are through the

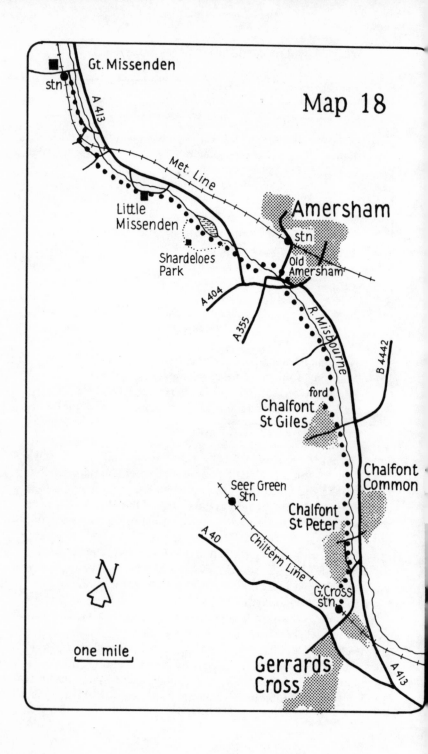

Map 18

Gt. Missenden
stn
A 413
Met. Line
Little
Missenden
Shardeloes
Park
A 404
A 355
Amersham
stn
Old
Amersham
R. Misbourne
B 4442
ford
Chalfont
St Giles
Chalfont
Common
Seer Green
Stn.
Chalfont
St Peter
A 40
Chiltern Line
G. Cross
stn
N
one mile
Gerrards
Cross
A 413

village and almost to the A413. Here you will find a FP on the right by Toby's Farm (NB You will already have passed one FP opposite the pub, which you should ignore.) The correct path goes ESE across a meadow, coming quite quickly back to the river which it follows for a good mile across Shardeloes Park. The lake at Shardeloes is not a natural water, but was created by Humphry Repton to complement the Palladian mansion built by Robert Adam for Sir William Drake in 1776, which you will soon see crowning the rise on your right.

The OS map shows part of the path edging the bank of the lake, but only if the lake is full does the path follow the shoreline; when the water level is low the path will be some distance from the edge. In any case please keep to the path through Shardeloes Park. The house at Shardeloes is now occupied as apartments and the park is owned and maintained by the leaseholders. Our right as walkers is only to follow the footpath, not to wander in the park or picnic beside the lake. However, it *is* our right to walk on the footpath, so proceed to the lodge gates and cross the drive to take up the footpath again on the far side.

There is a meeting of paths here; one goes on up the drive for Mop End (and will be met again later), but our path maintains roughly the south-east direction we have been following since Little Missenden to come out quite soon behind the houses in Amersham old town. Turn left when you encounter a paved path, and you will emerge in the middle of the High Street.

Take time for a pause here to visit a pub or tearoom, or just to spend a little time taking in the beauties of the town before proceeding along the High Street as far as the lovely old building that was once Bury Mill, one of the eleven mills on the Misbourne, and is now Ambers of Amersham. Cross the road here, and, opposite the Chequers, east of the petrol station, a footpath will take you via a stile back to the river bank again.

Ahead a new bridge takes the Amersham bypass over both footpath and river, after which the route continues more rurally for half a mile beside the river before crossing to the west bank at a ford and footbridge on the approach to Quarrendon Farm. It then keeps to the west bank for another 2 miles, to the outskirts of Chalfont St Giles.

This is a very pleasant walk: the river flowing broad and shallow, trees overhanging banks where celandines grow in spring, a gentle swell of meadowland rising to the right, and away to the left traffic humming along the busy A413, just far enough off to give you a cheerful feeling of escape from it all.

At the ford by Chalfont Mill, 2 miles from the bridge at Quarrendon, the footpath leaves the river for Chalfont St Giles village. So pass the ford without crossing it, and carry on a few yards along the lane, keeping in the same direction, until the lane becomes a footpath again. Still proceeding ESE, you will soon come behind houses and thence to the village.

Here the Misbourne feeds the village duckpond, a small part of the charm of Chalfont St Giles, which is complemented by old shops and cottages around the village green, several pubs (with a nice garden behind Merlin's Cave), a restored thirteenth-century church and the museum at Milton's cottage (described in greater detail during Walk no. 16).

If you have left a car at Great or Little Missenden you might think it prudent to return now by the same route. Those who have come by rail might find it easier to continue along the river another 2 miles to Chalfont St Peter, where a further mile will take them on to Gerrards Cross station on the Chiltern line to return to Marylebone. This is only of use if you have started from London, as although both the Chiltern line and the Metropolitan line start from Marylebone that is their only point of connection.

To continue to St Peter, then, cross the main road at St Giles village to go through the archway in the shops that leads to the church; but instead of entering the churchyard keep to the narrow path to the right of the lychgate to encircle the church precincts. This will bring you to the river again, to take up a path via a stile on the right which gives onto the field on the near side of the fence. This footpath will go through an orchard before it returns to the river bank, but from St Giles it follows the course of the river, though not always closely, all the way to St Peter, where it emerges in the village centre between the church and the Greyhound inn.

In years past the main street of Chalfont St Peter crossed the Misbourne at a ford here. That was in the days before the redevelopment, when the Greyhound still looked like a coaching inn. Now the coaching arch has been blocked up to make a dining room, and the river culverted under the A413 and the new shopping precinct. It is possible to pick up the river again later for a short distance, and there is a footpath where it flows through Chalfont Park, but for the most part the river bank is inaccessible between here and Denham, so our walk along the Misbourne ends at Chalfont St Peter.

For Gerrards Cross station, take the road to the right of the church, between the White Hart and The Poachers. Keep along here for under half a mile, bearing right at the roundabout into Packhorse Road where a signpost points plainly to 'Gerrards Cross'. When you come to the shopping centre you will also come to the railway station.

Walkers who start from Amersham Metropolitan station should follow the instructions below. Turn left on leaving the main station entrance to pass under the bridge at the corner and proceed downhill, following the road for 100 yards or so before crossing to enter the wood at the marked FP opposite.

The FP goes SSW through Parsonage Wood for a scant half mile and leads to a walkway beside St Mary's church, which emerges by the Memorial Gardens in the High Street. Turn left (east) along the High Street to pick up the river path opposite the Chequers.

Never so pretty as the Chess Valley Walk, this route along the Misbourne is most worthwhile for the lovely villages along the way: the mellow intimacy of Little Missenden: Old Amersham's quite spectacular buildings and market hall, and the twin villages of St Giles and St Peter, one a well-preserved village still and the other now a modern town with all that implies. All this, combined with the river walk, makes for an interesting day.

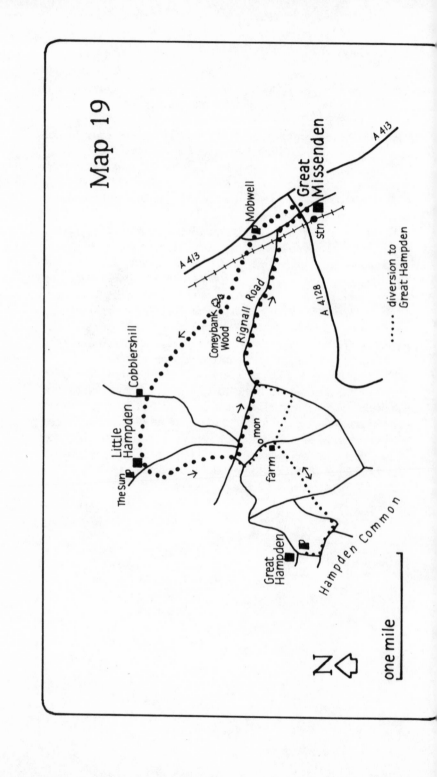

Map 19

Walk 19

**Great Missenden station – Mobwell – Coneybank Wood – Cobblers
Hill – Little Hampden – Great Missenden**

(8 miles)

ALTERNATIVES
From Little Hampden to Great Missenden via Honor End Farm
and Hotley Bottom
(6 miles)
Diversion to Great Hampden from Honor End Farm
(extra 3 miles)

OS map 165
Sketch map 19

[P]Link Road carpark, Great Missenden GR 894014
Black Horse at Mobwell (for customers) GR 891021
Station: Great Missenden (Met. line from Marylebone)

This next walk starts from the source of the Misbourne at Mobwell and gives an opportunity to see something of the farming
country around Great Missenden, including Honor End Farm at
Prestwood which is the piece of land for which John Hampden
refused to pay his tax assessment (twenty shillings, old money; but
that in 1634).

Turn left on leaving the station yard at Great Missenden, or
right from Link Road carpark, and proceed NNW along the road
for a good half mile, ignoring the two forks to the left leading to
Prestwood & Hampden, to arrive at the Black Horse at Mobwell.
(This is the home of the Black Horse Ballooning Society; on
summer evenings and weekends members meet in the field here to
launch their multi-coloured hot air balloons – a grand sight.)

The Misbourne rises in the pond opposite the inn, where a stile
gives onto a meadow.

There is also a footpath to Mobwell from Great Missenden, for which you should turn slightly right on leaving the station yard to walk up past Link Road carpark to the FP signposted left across fields. Keep well over to the right, near the hedge, after crossing the stile into the next field, ignoring the cutting under the A413 and the FP sign beside it, and coming instead to another stile in the hedge at the far end of the field, where you will find the Black Horse ahead of you. I wouldn't recommend this path as the going is lumpy and uneven, but for the fact that the hawthorn hedge that borders the road has a mass of rabbit-holes at its foot and the little chaps leap about all over the place. Also, the damp grass at the hedge bottom is smothered with blue and bronze bugle.

From Mobwell, then, go over the stile opposite the inn and on across the field, under the railway, to where the path plainly goes WNW to the right of the tree ahead. Make towards the hedge, where you ignore the stile to go instead through a conspicuous gap 50 yards to the right of it, onto a ploughed field. Here you go sharply up a bank, to keep left around the field edge and into Coneybank Wood. After only half a mile west and NNW through this wood, which is glorious with bluebells in spring and very pleasant at any time of year, the woodland path ends at a crossing track.

Here you turn left to continue north-west for two-thirds of a mile to Cobblers Hill, crossing a farm road shortly before emerging in Kings Lane, opposite twin signposts to Little Hampden. The left-hand sign points a bridleway to the church and Manor Farm, the right-hand one a footpath to the Rising Sun. Take the footpath, which after a north-westerly start soon goes due west for half a mile to the end of the road at Little Hampden – ever a favourite spot.

This is one village that has changed little since the Second World War: church, farms, cottages and inn all bunched together at the end of the no-through road with only footpaths, apart from the one long lane, to connect them to the world beyond.

Walk no. 6 gives directions for walking on through the wood (marked 'Little Hampden Common' on the OS map) to Dunsmore and thence to Wendover: not the best of paths, nowadays, thanks to all the horses that have been there before you. But our aim now is to return to Great Missenden, so turn downhill along the lane from the Sun to a footpath signposted along a track on the right, past The Croft and Cherry Tree Cottage, to a field path. Here, ignoring the path ahead to Warren Wood, you turn sharp left to pass Little Hampden Farm and proceed, at first between fences, back to Rignall Road.

Now you have a choice, either to turn left (east) where a 2½ mile tramp along the verge will return you to Great Missenden station, passing as you go Smithy Cottage on the left, still in use as a smithy, and on the right the gatehouses to the Hampden Estate, affectionately known as the Pepper Boxes.

Alternatively you can take the diversion to Honor End Farm and Hotley Bottom, for which you should cross the road on leaving the field path to go south along the paved lane opposite. Within 400 yards you will come to the Hampden Memorial on the left and Honor End Farm on the right. Opposite the farm a footpath goes east through Lodge Wood for another 400 yards to come to another paved lane at Hotley Bottom. (A little way up the lane here at Hotley Top the poet and essayist J.H.B. Peel, still remembered with affection by many Daily Telegraph *readers, lived for some years at Bield Cottage.)*

Turn left onto this paved lane, where a short walk will take you through the settlement at Hotley Bottom back to Rignall Road, to turn right for Great Missenden as described above.

There is an opportunity to visit Great Hampden in Walk no. 9, but it can be added to this walk by taking the southerly footpath from behind Honor End Farm, which soon turns south-west across fields to cross a lane and continue west and south-west to Great Hampden. You should emerge at a road junction; turn right, but ignore the road on your right, and instead cross over to skirt Hampden Common in a north-westerly direction for about 500 yards, when you will see the handsome inn sign belonging to the Hampden Arms. This diversion will add 2 miles to the walk. If it is a summer Sunday you might see cricket on the Common.

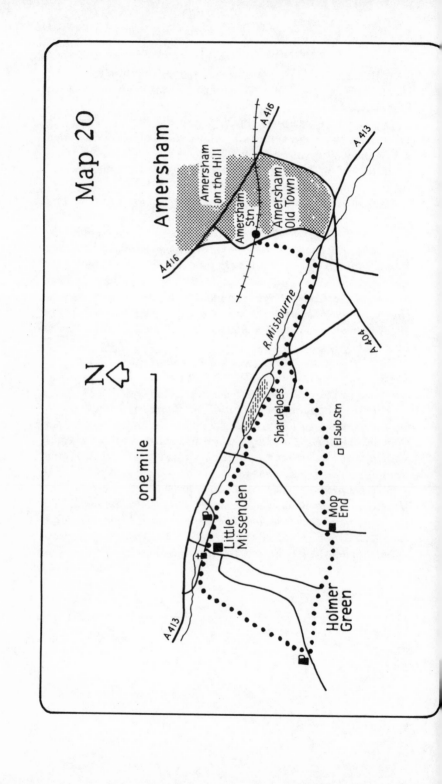

Map 20

Amersham

N

one mile

A 416

Amersham on the Hill

Amersham Stn

Amersham Old Town

A 416

A 413

R. Misbourne

A 404

Shardeloes

□ El Sub Stn

Little Missenden

Mop End

A 413

Holmer Green

Walk 20

Amersham station – Shardeloes – Little Missenden – Holmer Green – Mop End – Amersham

(10½ miles)

ALTERNATIVE
Start from Amersham old town
(9 miles)

OS map 165
Sketch map 20

P Behind bus garage in old Amersham GR 962973
Station: Amersham (Met. line from Baker St.)

This next walk, starting from the Metropolitan line station at Amersham on the Hill, gives a chance at the start for a good look at Amersham old town, a place already in existence in 1086 when it was listed as having 'two Mills on the Misbourne'. Mill House stands over the river at the west end of the High Street, a splendid building in chequered brick opposite the Drake Almshouses, and at the London end the former Bury Mill now houses a first-class Couturiers, Ambers of Amersham. There is a tiny window inside here through which part of the old mill machinery can be seen, and the millstream rushing under the building. Between these two mills Amersham High Street is one long line of history. The medieval church of St Mary is particularly fine inside and out. In addition to the many monuments (Pevsner says St Mary is 'richer in noteworthy monuments than any other church in the County except for Chenies & the Bedford Chapel'), you will see inside a collection of fifteenth-century floor tiles thought to have been made nearby at Penn, and behind the altar a modern nativity scene painted in 1988 by D.C. Morris.

Little Missenden, which you will come to later in the walk, is better yet, having the good fortune to lie along a side road away from the traffic. A winding village street, a Jacobean manor house, an unrestored eleventh-century church in flint and clunch – it is almost too good to be true.

From Amersham station the route goes down to the old town by a footpath through Parsonage Wood. Turn left on leaving the main station entrance to pass under the bridge at the corner and proceed downhill, following the road for 100 yards or so before crossing to enter the wood at the marked FP opposite.

The FP goes SSW through Parsonage Wood for a scant half mile and leads to a walkway beside St Mary's church, which emerges by the Memorial Gardens in the High Street. Turn right here towards the old town Hall, which stands across the carriageway, and follow the High Street until the houses end, continuing then along the verge of the A413 to the gates of Shardeloes Park.

We now have to negotiate the new Amersham bypass to reach Shardeloes, so cross to the left-hand (south) pedestrian path where the aptly-named Broadway begins to narrow (in fact cross sooner, to take a good look at the Drake Almshouses set round their little courtyard), and continue on past Little Shardeloes until the bypass comes in on the left. If the traffic is heavy or you have children in the party, instead of crossing here you can continue for another 100 yards to where the Misbourne is culverted under the two roads, where you will find a pleasant walkway beside the river.

Shardeloes, which you can see crowning the rise ahead, is a Palladian mansion built in 1766 for Stiff Leadbetter (marvellous names these people had) and later altered by Robert Adam. Our FP goes right (west) off the drive past the cricket pavilion. As mentioned elsewhere, this is a private park maintained at the cost of the several Shardeloes tenants, so please keep to the footpath as it goes beside the lake and then along the riverbank for a good 2 miles to emerge onto the road in Little Missenden village at Toby's Farm, 50 yards south-west of the Crown free house.

Little Missenden is Amersham old town all over again, but more intimate and without the shops, cars or bustle. Two useful pubs, a Jacobean manor house, church begun before the Conquest, winding road, river running by – all make this village a treat. Walk westwards (left) through the village and at the end, beyond the church and school, a footpath goes left up three wooden steps to cross a field still westwards and join a bridle path.

Turn left onto this path and follow it uphill due south through

Coleman's Wood for a little over a mile, to the outskirts of Holmer Green. This village has been drastically developed since the Second World War and has swollen to several times its original size, but there is still a good pub and still cricket on the green in summer. The FP enters the village at Penfold Lane, where you turn right, then left down Winters Way for about 200 yards. When the road forks, take the left-hand fork into a *cul de sac*; at the end you will find the FP continuing eastwards for a little less than a mile to the hamlet of Mop End. It goes a bit downhill, then up again, then crosses a lane above Beamond End, then a bridleway, finally taking up a green path diagonally across plough to come out onto the roadway at Mop End.

At Mop End the FP crosses another lane to continue along the bridleway by Griffin Cottage, once the Griffin Inn which had a tea garden much favoured by ramblers; sadly the inn is now a private house, so tea must await your return to Amersham where you will have marked down one or two places as you came through earlier.

From Mop End the bridleway proceeds east through Rough Park to skirt the electricity sub-station (they do find the oddest sites for these things) and continues very pleasantly back to Shardeloes Park where it rejoins the main drive, roughly where you left it.

6 The Long-Distance Footpaths

There are three waymarked long-distance routes in the Chilterns: the Ridgeway LDFP, the North Bucks Way and the Oxfordshire Way, the first being a designated LDFP route waymarked and tended by the Countryside Commission, and the other two being amenity routes waymarked and tended by the Ramblers' Association and other local bodies.

All make for good walking, but in some cases the lesser-known routes are a better bargain, being less 'walked out' than the officially designated path. The routes of all three are given in this chapter, starting with the best known first.

Walk 21 – The Ridgeway LDFP

Ivinghoe Beacon – Steps Hill – Clipper Down – Pitstone Hill –
Tring Gap – Tring Park – Hastoe Cross – Wendover Woods –
Hale Woods – Wendover – Coombe Hill – Lodge Hill – Chequers
– Kimble Hill – Whiteleaf Hill – Dame Lys – Ewelme Park –
Grim's Ditch – Mongewell Park – North Stoke – Cleve – Goring

(45 miles approx)

ALTERNATIVE
Finish via the Icknield Way

OS maps 165, 175 and 164

Following the completion of the Pennine Way in 1965, the early
1970s saw a spate of LDFPs opened: the Pembrokeshire Coast
Path in 1970, Offa's Dyke Path in 1971, North Downs Way and
South Downs Way in 1972, then in 1973 the Ridgeway, beaten by a
short head by the Southwest Coast Peninsular Path.

Rather more than half of the Ridgeway's 85 miles is in the
Chilterns; the rest follows the Oxfordshire (formerly Berkshire)
and Wiltshire downs. In the Chilterns the Ridgeway LDFP runs
for some 45 miles from Ivinghoe Beacon (GR 962168) to the
Thames at Goring, very largely along or just below the crest of the
hills. The idea for such a designated route was hatched by
members of the Ramblers' Association as long ago as 1942 when
the Pennine Way was still being fought for. It was to be thirty years
before their pipe dream was realized and the Ridgeway
Long-Distance Footpath officially opened at a ceremony held on
Coombe Hill in September 1973.

This LDFP is waymarked by the Countryside Commission with
the same symbols as are used for all the officially designated LDFPs:
white-painted acorns (the LDFP symbol), on stiles, gates and
fenceposts along the way, oak signposts with the acorn and the
name of the route carved in raised letters, and low stone plinths,
again with the acorn and the name of the route incised on the stone.

The Countryside Commission was formed to implement the provisions of the National Parks & Counryside Act of 1949, its principal duties being the designation of National Parks and Areas of Outstanding Natural Beauty (AONBs), together with the promotion of leisure activities and the protection of the countryside in general. The Commission was empowered to mark out long-distance routes for walkers and riders, and one of its first tasks in this connection was to record all public rights of way in England and Wales.

As designated, the Ridgeway LDFP starts from the Trig point on Ivinghoe Beacon, marked on the map as 'Beacon Hill'. It then follows the ridge westwards over Steps Hill, Clipper Down and Pitstone Hill, descending at the Tring Gap to make its way across Tring Park to Hastoe Cross and proceed through Wendover Woods, Hale Woods and along Hogtrough Lane into Wendover. After a short stretch along Wendover High Street, the path goes on over Coombe Hill and Lodge Hill to cross the Chequers estate. You can see Chequers from the footpath, but be warned and don't move in too close; a fellow writer found himself answering questions at Aylesbury police station in the early 1980s after straying too far from the path in order to take photographs.

From Chequers continue over Kimble Hill to Cadsdean Road, where the route passes in front of the Plough Inn (hurrah!) and turns steeply up through the beech woods to Whiteleaf Hill. This is one of the best stretches of the whole walk, particularly if you remember to cross the greensward ahead as you emerge through the gate onto Whiteleaf Hill, instead of immediately following the LDFP to the left. Then you will come to where Whiteleaf Cross is carved deep into the chalk on the north-west face of the hill. The cross itself is best seen from afar. It is said to be visible from 40 miles away on a clear day; but standing beside this best known of Chiltern hill figures one gets a marvellous view north and west over the Oxfordshire plain.

The history of Whiteleaf Cross is not know. The first possible record is in a Charter of 903 which mentions a 'boundary mark', but the first undisputed mention is in an Act of Parliament of George IV's time commanding that Whiteleaf Cross be kept in good order and regularly cleaned, and laying upon the owners of the Hampden Estate the responsibility for doing so. The Cross is now officially an ancient monument and presumably the onus is upon the Ministry of Works, now, to see to the cleaning.

Signposted from Whiteleaf down to Princes Risborough, the Path skirts that town to the south and follows the Wycombe road for a quarter of a mile before branching west on a lane to Shootacre Corner, where it crosses the Railway Line and follows a footpath due south for nearly a mile before turning west again. Thence it goes gloriously on over Lodge Hill to Wainhill and Chinnor. (There is more than one Lodge Hill and more than one Beacon Hill, too, in the Chilterns.)

This is another fine stretch of walking country, high, clear and windswept with the ground dropping sharply away to the south to show Chinnor, hundreds of feet below on the valley floor, with wisps of white smoke drifting lazily from the tall chimneys of the cement works. Who was it said that 'Distance lends enchantment to the view'?

Now the Path follows the straight track of the disused railway for best part of three miles, bypassing Chinnor and a number of pretty villages, to pass under the M40 in its own special tunnel and go on along the same straight path past Lewknor, Shirburn, Pyrton and Watlington. Don't try to see Shirburn Castle, marked on the map; it is in private hands and never open to the public; but do take note of Dame Lys Farm when you come to it along the green way, to the south of Watlington. This lovely old farmhouse was named for Dame Alice, Duchess of Suffolk, who once owned all the land here, having inherited it in her own right. Dame Alice's quite remarkable tomb and effigy are in the church at Ewelme, a lovely church in itself, built with a central nave, low, spreading north and south aisles and a squat western tower. Inside, the great east window and the plain glass of the clerestory lend light to all the treasures contained, which include a most elaborate 10 foot high font cover and the memorials of the Chaucer family. The Manor of Ewelme was inherited by Dame Alice from her father Thomas Chaucer, son of Geoffrey of the *Canterbury Tales*.

There is a feeling of antiquity to this stretch of the LDFP past Dame Lys; its age needs no telling. The boot falls upon the ground with a hollow thud, the trees close in, and when the old farmhouse appears hard on the edge of the footpath, bygone centuries claim you. The map shows a number of interconnecting tracks and green lanes here, as well as the more recently plotted Oxfordshire Way, which crosses the Ridgeway LDFP east of Watlington.

The Ridgeway turns due south after North Farm, a mile on past Dame Lys, leaving behind the green tracks of Hollandtide Bottom which runs from Berrick Salome to Brightwell Baldwin; Turner's Green Lane connecting Brightwell Baldwin with Britwell Salome, and Rumbold's Lane which doesn't quite join Ewelme to Chalgrove. Hollandtide Bottom is said to be a pre-Roman route, and it might be worth noting this area for exploration at a later date.

Having turned due south after North Farm, the path passes beside Swyncombe church before bearing west again for Ewelme Park, then south towards Nuffield, which it skirts to pick up the line of Grim's Ditch and follow that in a straight line westwards for the best part of 4 miles to the Thames at Mongewell Park. Here it makes a last turn south to follow the river bank through North Stoke and Cleve to the end of the Chiltern Ridgeway at Goring.

Grim's Ditch is an ancient earthworks marked in many places on the map of the Chilterns. It has exercised the imaginations of writers and historians for many years, and has been placed in period from pre-history to Roman times. With the more accurate dating methods now available to us, scientists have been able to date it at around AD 800 give or take a hundred years or so. In places as much as 40 feet wide and 30 deep, Grim's Ditch has been variously described as a defensive earthworks, a boundary marker, a fire-break, a device to keep animals from straying, or the work of the devil. It seems to be a case of 'you pays your money and you takes your choice'.

The route of the LDFP around Nuffield is not the best part of the way, and an alternative is to follow the Icknield Way from North Farm. Where the LDFP turns due south, the Icknield Way continues on south-west to become a paved road at Cow Common, branching south from a five-way junction at Beggarsbush Hill to cross Grim's Ditch and peter out into a green road again at Drunken Bottom, continuing thus the remaining 4 miles to Goring. I admit to a preference for this route, if only for the place names. It is less obviously interesting than that chosen for the LDFP, but has a great deal more atmosphere. It was with no surprise that I learned recently that aerial photographs had revealed the ditches of Bronze Age barrows beside this stretch of the Icknield Way, near Lonesome Farm. On this route, too, you pass within half a mile of the church at Ewelme mentioned earlier, making the diversion not only possible but imperative.

The Ridgeway is more than just a long-distance footpath. Where it runs along or just below the ridges of the hills from Ivinghoe to Tring, from Wendover to Whiteleaf and from Wainhill to Swyncombe downs the LDFP follows the route of the Icknield Way, the ancient track that once rode the chalk ridges south-westerly across the bottom of England from the North Norfolk coast to Salisbury Plain, and on to where the river Exe flows into the sea. Its antiquity is shown by the burial mounds, hill forts, temples and other relics found beside the way. In the Chiltern section, particularly, 'way' is a good description for this old route, as it is not one path but many, all making in the same general direction.

There is the Upper Icknield Way, which more or less followed the spring line; the Lower Icknield Way, now mainly paved and surviving as the B4009 which runs in the valley, and a high footpath along or just below the ridge, most of which has been adopted for the LDFP. Such parallel ways were defined by the feet of those that walked them, going high on the hills in one season, low in the valley in another, seeking only to find the safest ground, summer or winter.

Directions over cultivated ground can be specific: 'Go to the corner of the next field and cross the stile to emerge onto a lane, where turn left for half a mile before proceeding along Pound Street' makes sense when all those places are readily identifiable. In wide open country it is enough to say 'make to where the sun sets' or 'to the clump of trees on the horizon', and in this way not one path is made but many, all with the same destination.

As Edward Thomas wrote in his book *The Icknield Way* published in 1913, 'The first roads were made by men following herds, either as hunters or as herdsmen ... The great road of pilgrimage from Damascus to Mecca is not a made road, but composed of parallel strands of old, hollow camel paths...'. And so he found this old route through the Chilterns to be the parallel strands of many paths made over the centuries. He mentions three distinct routes in his book: the footpath on the ridge and two cart-tracks known as the Upper and Lower Icknield Way. His brief being to write about the Icknield Way, he turns back having reached Goring because 'I had to go back to the forking of the Way and follow the Lower road from Ivinghoe'.

Edward Thomas called his book a 'hack work', because it was commissioned as a series of newspaper articles. But the American poet Robert Frost found the prose so enchanting that he encouraged the writer to release the poetry within him, and by the time Edward Thomas was killed in Flanders four years later he had written and published enough to establish himself as a poet of some magnitude.

He did not enjoy the solitary trek by pony cart through Norfolk and the Chilterns, and *The Icknield Way* is suffused, in consequence, with a poetic melancholy that makes it memorable reading. If you plan to walk the Ridgeway, do try to read this book first. It is issued in paperback by Wildwood House, and will add greatly to your enjoyment, though you will find things very different in the Chilterns today – different even from what they were when the LDFP was first conceived in the 1940s.

In the early days of the LDFP walking the Ridgeway was an adventure. None of us knew the route, the paths were fresh and unexplored and still firm and green underfoot, and the white-painted acorns, stone plinths and signposts were new and easy to find. Thousands of pairs of boots had not yet tramped the path into the scar across the countryside that it was to become. I remember one stretch near Tring which had been hacked through the middle of a broad hedge; there were raw stumps and wood chippings everywhere and one had to step very carefully to avoid tripping on the tree roots left behind. But this was an isolated example of unpleasantness. Most of the way was over springy turf on the crest of the hills or on the leafmould of centuries in the beech woods, routes that were to degenerate over the years into bare chalk slides and quagmires. Fortunately nature is forgiving, and the National Trust, which owns much of the chalk uplands, together with the Countryside Commission have done their best to give nature a helping hand. Diversions are signposted from time to time to allow badly worn stretches of the path to regenerate, and the worst areas of erosion on the hills are patched with plastic netting, to hold a surface over the chalk, and reseeded with boot-defying grasses.

Ordnance Survey Landrangers 165, 175 and 164 cover the routes of the LDFP and the Icknield Way through the Chilterns, marking them 'Ridgeway' or 'LDP' in the case of the LDFP, and 'Upper Icknield Way' or 'Lower Icknield Way' in the case of the older path. There is also a special set of overprinted sheets available from the Countryside Commission which marks out the route of the LDFP in its entirety.

Apart from the maps, there are several good pocket guides to the Ridgeway LDFP on the market, written to help the walker. Alan Charles's *Ridgeway Path*, issued by Countryside Books, is one of the best. Mr Charles leads you almost every step of the way, and also offers advice on accommodation and public transport. A simpler guide in map form, but still with notes on transport, accommodation, and items of interest along the route, is H.D. Westacott's *Practical Guide to Walking The Ridgeway Path*.

Walk 22 – The Oxfordshire Way LDFP

Henley – No Man's Hill – Middle Assendon – Bix Bottom –
Warburg reserve – Maidensgrove – Pishill – Christmas
Common – Pyrton

(12 miles approx.)

At about the time the Ridgeway LDFP was designated in 1973, someone in the CPRE came up with the idea of a long-distance path to link the two adjacent Areas of Outstanding Natural Beauty, the Chilterns and the Cotswolds. The path was to be called the Oxfordshire Way.

The idea was taken up by the Oxfordshire Field Paths Society and, once more, the Ramblers' Association, this time the Oxford Area branch. Between them their members tramped out and waymarked a 65 mile route of linked footpaths from the banks of the Windrush at Bourton-on-the-Water to the banks of the Thames at Henley.

Roughly half the route, that part south and east of the River Thame (not 'Thames') is in the Chilterns. The River Thame gathers in the Vale of Aylesbury and wanders south and west towards the town of Thame, joining there with Dad Brook and Cuttle Brook before meandering westwards through watermeadows across Oxfordshire. At Holton Mill, below Waterperry, the Thame turns due south, flowing away to lose itself at last in the great Thames at Dorchester.

The Thame makes a rough boundary, but it is the vernacular that marks the true change from Chilterns to Cotswolds. When roofs of pale Stonesfield slate and walls of mellow stone replace thatch and rounded, whitewashed cottages you will know you have left the Chilterns behind you.

A comprehensive guide with route maps, information on transport and accommodation and detailed instructions for those not good with maps is available from the Oxfordshire County Council, County Hall, Oxford (£1.50, in advance); and, as this guide will tell you, the proper start to the walk is at Bourton-on-the-

Water in Gloucestershire, where it 'leaves the Windrush and makes for the village green' to climb 800 feet to Wyke Beacon before dropping down into Oxfordshire.

The Way crosses all the five belts of terrain that make up Oxfordshire: the Cotswold limestones, Oxford clay vale, Corallian Heights, Gault clay vale, and finally the Chiltern chalk. It is a unique journey through one of the most attractive and varied counties in England. From places such as Shipton under Wychwood, Charlbury and Stonesfield, and following in part such ancient routes as the Fosse Way and Akeman Street, the Way comes into the Chilterns around Pyrton, a village of timber and thatch and warm red brick. John Hampden, the Patriot, married his first wife at Pyrton on midsummer day in 1619, walking his bride to the church from her father's newly completed manor house close by. Pyrton Manor stands today as it did then, but the church was zealously restored by the Victorians.

Pyrton's Plough Inn is newly golden thatched and retains its heavily timbered, low-ceilinged public rooms, and makes a fitting end to a good 12 mile walk from Henley. For it is from Henley, for the purposes of this book, that the walk will start.

From the Angel on Henley Bridge, walk up Hart Street opposite to Bell Street, first on the right, and follow on along Northfield Road until you pass the Youth Hostel on your left and tennis courts on your right. A little way past the tennis courts, at GR 756834, a stile right gives onto a footpath bearing north-east, which for the official guide is the finish, but for us is the start, of the Oxfordshire Way.

Running beside a hedge, the path rises steeply at first up No Man's Hill, which if you look back gives an excellent view of Henley and the river, and continues north-east for the best part of 2 miles, to turn west after crossing a byroad for the village of Middle Assendon. Bar food is available in the pub here; but come off it, you've only just started!

At Middle Assendon the route follows the Stonor road north for 500 yards to turn sharp left at Bix Hall Farm and follow the rough track west for half a mile, then north-west again past Little Bixbottom Farm to Bix Bottom. Bix village lies today on the busy A423, but once it was here in Bix Bottom, and to the left of the Way before Valley Farm is reached, and where a bridlepath goes due west to Nettlebed, there are in a field the remains of the former parish church of St James, abandoned in 1875. The church is said to have been part-Norman, and certainly Bix is mentioned in the *Domesday Book* as 'Held by Hugh from Walter Gifford'. Walter Gifford acquired great chunks of Oxfordshire and Buckinghamshire after the Conquest.

What caused the demise of old Bix and the rise of the new settlement seems not to be known; some writers attribute it to the Plague, but the church in the new settlement wasn't built until 1874 and the old church was abandoned the following year, which makes it a bit late for the Plague. Perhaps it was just a question of the new settlement being so much more accessible.

After Bix Bottom the track becomes a FP, continuing to rise gently into the lovely mixed woodlands of BBONT's Warburg Reserve where you might see fallow deer or muntjac, adders or grass snakes; though you are unlikely to see the badgers and foxes that also live here. The Reserve is 247 acres of woodland, scrub and chalk grassland bought by public subscription in 1968, with the help of a donation from the World Wildlife Fund, and managed by BBONT. Broad grassy rides and open areas of scrubland lighten the pine plantations and heavy mixed woodlands which clothe the steep slopes, and in these clearings a rich chalk flora flourishes. The Trust's Handbook tells of seventeen species of orchid found here, including Fly orchid, Greater and Lesser Butterfly, Bee and Frog orchids, and Green Helleborine, also Solomon's Seal and Adder-stongue Fern. There is a resident warden with a house on the Reserve, and all visitors are requested to keep to the footpaths.

BBONT manages upwards of fifty reserves. For a guide to the Reserve at Bix and details of conducted tours, contact BBONT at 3 Church Cowley Road, Rose Hill, Oxford. If you promise to be good, they might let you become a member.

Just under 3 miles walking from Middle Assendon brings you to the tiny hamlet of Maidensgrove, described by H.J. Massingham writing in 1940 as 'the most remote hamlet in all the Chilterns'. Maidensgrove Scrubs, on the approach to the hamlet, he saw as a 'toy wilderness of pigmy oak and bracken on clay with flints, honeycombed by little turfen paths winding snake wise down the hillside'. He goes on to say 'The golden time to be in these woods ... is on a misty day in November when every tree is pale copper, and you can look over their heads down into the Bix valley, filled with a plumcoloured haze like grapebloom'.

After Maidensgrove the Way veers north-east then due north to the village of Pishill (formerly 'Peas Hill', apparently, which sounds a little more civilized). Pishill is little more than a pub and a pillarbox, but it has a south-west window in the church with modern glass by John Piper. It is less than 5 miles now to the end of the walk at Pyrton.

Follow the main street north through Pishill village, crossing the road that runs from Stonor in the east to Swyncombe in the west, and continue NNW until the track becomes a footpath again and skirts through the edge of College Wood, all bluebells in spring, to turn sharply east across a lane by Hollandridge Farm before turning back north-east once more. Wild duck sometimes roost on the ponds by Hollandridge Farm; strange how no bird so well expresses the joy of flying as this intrinsically ungainly bird. Only the skeins of honking, high-flying geese are more evocative of freedom.

Soon you are in deep woodland again for the 1½ miles to Christmas Common, following for much of the way a bridlepath along the valley bottom. Eventually the path rejoins Hollandridge Lane and emerges on the roadway at a farm entrance. For the village of Christmas Common walk 100 yards or so left (NNE still) along this road to a fork, where you turn back around this fork if you want to visit the village. There is nothing remarkable here, but a good pub with bar food and occasional buses to Henley or Watlington.

Back to the fork again, and the Way goes briefly on along the road to another fork, where it takes a rough track to the left of the right-hand road, which this time leads to Watlington. The Way leaves the road by a stile and crosses the field downhill to another stile diagonally left in the corner of a paddock. Here it comes onto a bridlepath past Pyrton Hill House which takes you first across the Ridgeway LDFP/Icknield Way, then in half a mile or so to the B4009, which leads on the left into Watlington. Cross this B4009 and continue another half mile up the lane opposite for Pyrton, keeping right when the land forks.

In the course of this last mile or so you will have passed from the Chilterns to the Oxfordshire Plain. Beeches and bluebells, flint and thatch are left behind after Pyrton in favour of more sober joys of the Gault clay vale. You could choose to continue the remaining 52 miles of the Oxfordshire Way, through such delightful places as

Rycote and Waterperry, Weston on the Green and Sturdy's Castle, Stonesfield (where the slates came from) and Wyck Rissington untouched by the centuries. But a description of the remainder of the Oxfordshire Way has no place in a book devoted to walking in the Chilterns.

The portion of the Oxfordshire Way here described can be followed on OS sheets 175 and 165, or on Pathfinder sheets SU68/78 (Henley) and SU69/79 (Watlington & Stokenchurch). There is no bus service to Pyrton at the time of writing; walkers who finish there should make their way back into Watlington for buses to Henley or for a taxi service.

Walk 23 – North Bucks Way

**Chequers Knap – Kimble Wick – Bishopstone – Hartwell –
Whaddon Hill – Eythrope Park – Waddesdon – Quainton**

(15 miles)

ALTERNATIVE
End at Waddesdon
(12½ miles)

Unlike the Ridgeway, the North Bucks Way is not designated as
an official Long-Distance Footpath, but it is marked on the new
Landranger series of OS maps. It was pioneered by members of
the Bucks & West Middx branch of the Ramblers' Association,
together with members of the North Bucks Rambling Club, in
1972. The waymarking is by yellow arrows on stiles and gateposts,
and we have to thank members of those organizations for keeping
the arrows bright and the hedges trimmed back. Only the Lord
and the weather can do anything about the going underfoot.

The 30 mile chain of footpaths starts on Chequers Knap above
Kimble, where the Ridgeway LDFP crosses, and ends within sight
of the new City of Milton Keynes. Unlike the Ridgeway, which
keeps for the most part to high ground away from habitation, the
NBW seeks out the villages, so that although a strong walker
might aim to walk the whole of it in the course of one long summer
day, the better part would be to take it more slowly, put up for a
night along the way, and enjoy the sights.

Right from the start all but the most incurious or those to whom
the district is thoroughly familiar could find themselves detained,
for the area around Chequers Knap is full of interest. There is an
Iron Age fort to the south on Pulpit Hill, and beyond it on the
chalk grasslands spotted and pyramidal orchids flourish in season,
while on the slopes north of the Knap is the forest of gnarled,
low-growing box trees of Kimble Warren and the deep deserted
coombe of Happy Valley.

This area around Chequers Knap is an SSSI, held on lease from the Chequers Estate by BBONT – the Berks, Bucks & Oxfordshire Naturalists' Trust. The Trust's Reserves Handbook lists walnut and wych elm among other trees in Happy Valley; green and great spotted woodpeckers, spotted flycatchers, finches in winter, and muntjac, badger and fox at all times.

On the hills to the north of Happy Valley is Cymbeline's Castle, the remains of a green defended encampment where Cunobelinus, King of the Britons, fought a last-ditch battle against the Romans ... and lost, alas – probably finished up walking to Rome in chains. To the east of this is the tree-crowned top of Beacon Hill, and farther east still the finger of the Boer War Monument on Coombe Hill, both visible for miles across the Vale of Aylesbury.

From the start on Chequers Knap (GR 830053) an obvious downhill path leads briefly north-west down to the road at Great Kimble. Here, not half a mile from the start, I urge you to stop again to see the unassuming little country church of St Nicholas which is one of the most historic sights in Buckinghamshire. Here was the meeting held at which John Hampden, 'Ship Money Hampden' to generations of schoolchildren, supported by his neighbours, defied King Charles I over what they decided was an illegally applied tax. Ship Money, instituted to supply the King's navy, was meant to apply only to ports and coastal towns; the King had no business applying it to farmers, who had plenty of taxes of their own thank you very much. John Hampden and his neighbours set out their refusal to pay, each signing the document with John Hampden at their head, and a framed copy of that document hangs in the church at Great Kimble. It was the start of the Civil War; who could pass it without a glance?

If you are interested in churches, a scant quarter of a mile north along the road here is All Saints Church, Little Kimble, a tiny thirteenth-century flint church with a bellcote, Jacobean pulpit and a series of medieval wall paintings.

There is no excuse to waste time for the next couple of miles as you go through the kissing gate and proceed north-west to the village of Kimble Wick. Here at Dodd's Charity Farm are the kennels of the Aylesbury Vale Hunt. There is nothing to see there, but the old farm house will stop you on sight: stark and angular, it shouts antiquity. The house resembles nothing so much as the fifteenth-century grammar school at Ewelme, along the Ridgeway in Oxfordshire. It is only a fraction of the size, but has the same rich, dark brick and tall chimneys, the same bare angularity. The Huntsman's wife, when asked, couldn't put a date to the building but spoke eloquently of age and atmosphere, of eerie attics and deep cellars, queerly shaped cupboards and uneven floors, steps up and steps down in odd places, and in the winter cold, iron cold.

Dodd's Charity makes both a curtain-raiser and a contrast to Bishopstone, a long 2 miles on and more picturesque, with timber frame and thatch. You could be ready for a snack at Bishopstone, at the Harrow, and this will be your last chance until the Bugle Horn at Hartwell, more modern, more popular and on the main road.

At Hartwell the Way goes briefly along the A418 beside the boundary wall to Hartwell House, where the immediate interest is in the unbelievably huge ammonites built into the perimeter wall, all dug locally from the chalk. Further interest is in Hartwell House itself, owned by the people of Buckinghamshire and used by them for a multitude of community activities including the annual Bucks show. But it was not always so. This Jacobean stone mansion was built to the order of Sir Thomas Lee in 1618, and remained in his family. Early in the nineteenth century Louis XVIII and his Court came to live for seven years in exile at Hartwell. The King, who was a scholar, enjoyed this quiet time, but his Queen found it impossibly dull and eased her boredom by knocking off the figure heads that decorated the balusters of the grand staircase, leaving a twentieth-century restorer to replace them with representations of G.K. Chesterton, Sir Winston Churchill, and other twentieth-century notables.

From Hartwell the route makes north up to Whaddon Hill Farm, and as you climb the view opens up to the right to reveal the county town of Aylesbury laid out before you. Until the 1960s this view was of a traditional market town settled around a spire-topped parish church, surrounded by meadows and farming country. Today the church and the Georgian streets that hem it in are dwarfed by the eleven-storey block of the County offices, and the eye is diverted from the centre by a mish-mash of multi-storey carparks, ringways and new estates. This is one view to which even distance can hardly lend enchantment.

After Whaddon Hill the route drops down north-west to cross a stream and make for the banks of the River Thame (not to be confused with its big brother, the Thames) – a waterway which notoriously leaves its shallow bed at the least encouragement, wandering across the watermeadows after heavy rains and forming great shallow lakes in wet winters. (Tip: wear boots.) A footbridge over a sluice takes the Way across the Thame to the Rothschild estates at Eythrope Park and Waddesdon: sleek and well-cared-for estates, with sturdy lodges and estate houses and anything but Buckinghamshire-style mansions. 'The Pavilion' built for Dame Alice de Rothschild comes into view on the right soon after the river is crossed, and later the impossible towers of Waddesdon Manor rise to the north-west, crowning shimmering walls of pale Bath stone.

Later the route passes the Five Arrows hotel in Waddesdon village, now a village pub and a good place for bar snacks, but originally built as a hunting lodge for Rothschild weekend guests. The five-arrows motif which appears on so many of the Rothschild buildings, both great and humble, in south Bucks is the Rothschild family crest and denotes the five brothers who founded the banking dynasty in the late eighteenth-century. Waddesdon Manor was given by the family to the National Trust, complete with all its contents. If you hold a National Trust card you might picnic in the park or make use of the tearooms, but if you try to 'take in' the manor it will cost you half a day, so much is there to see.

Waddesdon village, 12½ miles from the start, makes a good point to end the day's walk. Quainton, 2½ miles on, might be better for a number of reasons, but at Waddesdon there are buses connecting with Aylesbury and Bicester. Beyond Waddesdon, too, we can hardly pretend to be any longer in the Chilterns.

The hills ahead are not Chiltern hills, but part of the Purbeck-capped Portland Beds, causing the lower slopes of Quainton Hill to be pitted and humped with the spoil of long-abandoned quarries. However, it would be a shame to be so purist about territory as to miss the delightful village of Quainton, so short a distance ahead.

You come upon Quainton village suddenly from a path between houses: a hummocky green sloping up towards a windmill and the oldest market cross in Buckinghamshire. These lead the way to a church whose Victorian restorer left it with nave and aisles of Early English Gothic, with fourteenth-, fifteenth- and sixteenth-century brasses, and more monuments than any other church in the county. The church is bounded on the left by a Georgian rectory chequered with those blue bricks so familiar in the Chilterns, and on the right by a row of fine, dormered almshouses built in 1687 to the order of Richard Winwood for 'three poor men, widowers, to be called Brothers; and three poor women, widows, to be called Sisters'. The Winwood family monuments are found in the church. Four pubs, a chequered brick farmhouse and numerous timber-framed, thatched cottages are among the other joys to be found in Quainton, a village described by Sir Arthur Bryant as having the 'still unbroken peace of centuries'.

The Chiltern hills are now firmly left behind, but of the North Bucks Way a good half remains. It will take you, should you care to follow it, across the open fields of the Buckinghamshire countryside, past the thatched cottages in the lovely village of East Claydon, through Verney Junction, once a very important railway crossing but now no more than a pub serving snacks beside a rarely used railway line, and on across the Buckingham road to Whaddon Chase. Here in the Chase are the isolated villages of Great Horwood, Nash and Whaddon, lying in undulating pasturelands where you will find old inns and manor houses, village ponds and meandering brooks, until you come at last to the medieval highway leading to the new, modern city of Milton Keynes.

You can trace out the NBW on OS 1/50,000 Landrangers Nos. 165 and 152, or you can buy the pamphlet published by the Bucks and West Middx branch of the Ramblers' Association which describes the route almost step by step, guiding you through the tricky bits and telling you which buses to catch, etc. The pamphlet, entitled *The North Buckinghamshire Way* is available from enlightened booksellers or direct from the Ramblers' Association.

One other small point: at East Claydon it is worth going a mile (each way) off course to visit Claydon House, now in the care of the National Trust. This small, delightful Palladian house was home to Florence Nightingale in her declining years and in the first-floor museum there are a number of photographs, letters and effects of hers. Furthermore, the staircase and the ground-floor rooms deserve the description 'magnificent', while the history of the Verney family, with their Civil War connection, mirrors the history of Buckinghamshire. It is well worth a 2 mile diversion, but check first in your NT handbook to be sure the house is open. The opening dates at the time of writing are: April to October, Saturday to Wednesday 2–6pm, Bank Hol. Mon. 1–6pm, closed Good Friday.

7   A Walk Along the Thames

The only positive boundary to the Chilterns is to the south and west where the hills come down to the Thames, and where there is one last long-distance walk along the towpath.

You might think this the most straightforward walk. Here is the river, and the river has a towpath: impossible to go astray. So I thought when, some years ago, I set out from Chiswick Bridge to go as far as I could in the one week, aiming for the Oxfordshire watermeadows and the Scholar Gipsy's crossing at 'Bab-lock-hithe'. All went well as far as Shepperton, where the towpath crosses to the north bank to avoid the confluence with the River Wey. This was where I became aware of the complication of the missing Thames ferries.

Passage on the river, and on all our rivers, has been free since Magna Carta, but there was no right of way along the banks of the Thames until the Thames Commissioners were appointed in the late 1700s; one of their remits being to make and maintain a towpath. This was no easy task, as not only were there swamps and other natural barriers such as this confluence with the Wey, but by that time long stretches of the river bank were in private ownership. As a consequence the towpath came to be laid down now along the north bank, now along the south, as circumstance dictated, the crossings from one bank to another being effected by flat, shallow punts able to ferry across four barge horses as well as foot passengers and their goods.

The demise of these ferries involves intending towpath-walkers in annoying diversions away from the river along certain stretches, the most notable place in the Chilterns being at Temple Island above Marlow where a necessary diversion takes you from a particularly pleasant stretch of towpath on the north bank in favour of a road walk through Bisham. Once again we have the

Ramblers' Association to thank for waging a fifty-year battle to get rights of way established along the river, culminating with the opening of a bridge above Temple lock in the summer of 1989, so that a continuous walk from Putney to the river's source at Cricklade is now possible using the towpath for most of the way. A stage by stage guide to this route is available from the RA, entitled *The Thames Walk*. It is never easy to decide how much of this long-distance walk can be claimed for the Chilterns, but the 45 miles from Windsor to Goring, rather less than a third of the total distance, seems to qualify.

Walk 24

Eton – Maidenhead – Cliveden Reach – Cookham – Winter Hill –
Quarrybank Wood – Marlow – Henley – March Lock Island –
Lashbrook – Shiplake lock – Sonning – Reading – Mapledurham
lock – Pangbourne – Whitchurch – Goring

(46 miles approx.)

ADDITIONS
Marlow – Temple – (Hurley) – Bisham – Marlow
Hambleden – Woodend – Bacres – Colstrope – Hambleden
Hambleden – Henley – Craigwell House – Aston – Hambleden

Making a start at the pedestrian bridge which links Windsor and
Eton, the route turns left from the bridge and left again at the
Waterman's Arms to come to the towpath beyond the Eton
College boathouses. it keeps to the towpath then as far as
Maidenhead bridge, where the towpath crosses to the opposite
bank.

At Maidenhead the towpath follows the road alongside the river
until just past Boulters Lock, where it goes down to the riverbank
again to rejoin the towpath and give the walker an enjoyable tramp
around Cliveden Reach. On the approach to Cookham weir the
towpath crosses briefly to the north bank. *My Lady Ferry* once
plied here, and the ferry cottages can be seen on the opposite
bank, but the ferry being gone we must keep to the south bank and
take instead the woodland path leading to Mill Lane and the
A4094. At the main road the route goes right for Cookham, then
left before the bridge to go through the churchyard and back to the
riverbank again.

Now there are 1½ miles of good walking beside the river before
the towpath crosses to the north bank again at Spade Oak. We can
see the towpath clearly on the north bank going very pleasantly
through the watermeadows in the direction of Marlow, but call as
we may for the ferryman none will come, so we must stay on the
south bank once more, and make our way to Marlow over Winter

Hill and through Quarrybank Wood. This is really no hardship, as the route gives a fine view over the Chilterns from the top of Winter Hill. Take the path off left beyond the ferry cottage, and keeping the riverside cottages on your right follow the marked footpath to the corner of the field, where it bears left and over a stile to go diagonally right up the hillside. On reaching the road the route turns right again, and follows the road to the top of Winter Hill.

Leaving the broad hilltop, the route turns right along a gravel path beside Dial Place to take up a narrow FP alongside a house named Rivendell, keeping straight on when the path forks. At the road turn right, to take up a steep path leading down to Quarry Wood Road, where the route again bears right, over the bridge and past the Scouts Boating Centre. At the road bridge ahead a flight of steps on the left takes the route over the river to rejoin the towpath on the far bank, where a right turn will bring you, with a diversion round the weir, to Marlow. The two flights of steps which made this river crossing possible were constructed by members of the Ramblers' Association, but until the wooden bridge was built upstream in 1989 to replace the old *Temple Ferry* there was no point in following the towpath on from Marlow along the south bank, as it came eventually to a dead end. A diversion through Bisham was necessary involving a nasty crossing of the A404 and missing out Marlow altogether. In some ways I regret the loss of leafy Bisham with its twelfth-century church, pretty cottages, and chance of a quick one at the Bull, but this can be the subject of an independent walk and the new bridge does give a continuous 8 mile towpath walk from Marlow to Henley along what must be one of the prettiest stretches of the Thames.

At Henley the towpath crosses to the north bank again and the route follows the road briefly before crossing Hobbs Boathouse slipway to the riverbank. It goes over the wooden causeways at Marsh Lock Island then continues beside the river to the site of *Bolney Ferry*, where the towpath crosses to the far bank for a mile before returning to the north bank again at Lashbrook. There is no chance, of course, to cross at Bolney or Lashbrook, so a diversion along the north bank across a plank bridge, over a stile and on through two wicket gates brings us eventually to take a left fork between houses, then a right fork between hedges and across the railway line, where a footpath leads on to Shiplake station. Before the level crossing, turn up Mill Road for the best part of a mile, passing through the hamlet of Lashbrook, and at the T-junction with Mill Lane turn left towards the imposing house ahead, where a right turn beside a flint wall will bring you to Shiplake lock. The route rejoins the towpath here via a stile on the right, and without crossing the lock keeps close to the riverbank all the way to Sonning.

At Sonning Bridge the towpath crosses to the south bank, and again the route keeps to the riverbank, negotiating the confluence with the River Kennet on the old Horseshoe Bridge. The towpath then takes us right through Reading on an easy through-route that any motorist driving across that notoriously busy town would envy. 'Private' signs where the towpath passes the premises of Reading Marine Services you can ignore; no part of the Thames towpath is, or ever has been, 'private'. However, a little way ahead the towpath deserts us at the site of *Roebuck Ferry*, changing to the north bank for a mere 500 yards. So we must take the footbridge over the railway there and turn along the road to the steps down to Purley Park Estate. The narrow estate road around Purley Park leads right over another rail bridge to a track down to the river, where Mapledurham weir can be seen across the fields.

At Mapledurham lock the towpath returns to our side for a good 2 mile trot to Pangbourne. It is possible to continue on along the towpath beyond Pangbourne, but at Gatehampton Ferry, best part of 3 miles ahead, there is no crossing to the far bank. (Gatehampton Bridge, shown on the OS map, is a rail bridge only.) If we kept to the towpath here we would find ourselves with a long road walk into Streatley and quite miss the lovely river walk through Goring Gap. So it is best to leave the towpath at Pangbourne and cross the river by the toll bridge to Whitchurch (free to walkers, motorists pay 6p).

Take the main road northwards through Whitchurch village for about half a mile to where, at a left fork, a signpost points 'Bridleway to Goring, 3m'. The bridleway goes to Gatehampton Manor, and thence back to the river at *Gatehampton Ferry* where the towpath has at last crossed to our side ready to take us gloriously into Goring. This stretch, where the wooded banks come steeply down to the river, is exceptionally fine and makes a fitting end to the long walk.

With railway connections at Maidenhead, Cookham, Henley,

Shiplake, Reading, Pangbourne and Goring, this is an easy walk to complete in short stretches, though a stout walker could manage it comfortably in a weekend.

You will find the course of the river on OS 175, and the Nicholson/OS *Guide to the River Thames* is also useful. In addition to the towpath walk, the map shows plenty of good short walks taking in stretches of the riverbank; the walk through Bisham mentioned above is one. Follow the towpath south from Marlow suspension bridge towards Temple and cross at the handsome new timber bridge. On the far bank, continue away from Temple very briefly, 50 yards or so, to a narrow path going off left which emerges after some 300 yards onto a broad, leafy track.* Turn left again, and after half a mile this track becomes a paved roadway at Temple village. Keep to this paved road for another three-quarters of a mile, when sharp right then left turns will take you through Bisham and return you, in another 1½ miles, to Marlow bridge: a pleasant 4½ mile walk.

You could extend this by another 1½ miles by continuing along the towpath (after crossing the bridge at Temple) as far as Hurley, where a path leaves the river to pass Hurley Priory, and continue for some 200 yards before turning left onto that same broad track mentioned at * above. Along this track, incidentally, quite near to the hamlet at Temple, you will be confronted by a dank, narrow underpass. If this disconcerts you, it can be avoided by dodging round to the right and climbing up to cross the drive under which it passes, rejoining the track again on the left by a gate in the wall. Actually the underpass is usually quite dry and sweet, but if you come to it at dusk....

You won't want to miss Hambleden, a delightful village to the north of the A4155 between Marlow and Henley where there are several good walks, and where England's premier newsagent (and so much more), W.H. Smith, lies in the churchyard. There is a good public carpark on the left as you turn towards the village off the A4155. Leaving the carpark, and before you reach the village, a path goes off left up through Great Wood towards Woodend, turning sharply east after about 2 miles to Bacres and Colstrope, and back south by a woodland path to Hambleden village. Or you could take the bridlepath right, 200 yards north of the carpark, which emerges after half a mile in Hambleden village, goes briefly along the main street then makes off east again by the church for three-quarters of a mile to Hutton's Farm. Here a sharp right turn for 150 yards brings you to another bridlepath going off left (east) again, to turn back south when a paved lane is reached. This paved lane will take you through the hamlet of Rotten Row and back, after 1½ miles, to Mill Lane, where you should turn right for the carpark.

My own favourite is the route which takes in Hambleden Mill and the weir, follows the river along the Henley Regatta course and returns through Henley and Aston. Turn right from the carpark towards Hambleden Mill on the far side of the A4155, and take the altogether joyous walk across the duckboards that takes you over the river and the weir, then follow the towpath north-west for 3 magic miles to Henley. Without crossing the river, leave Henley by the A423 for some 500 yards to take the signposted path left up steps past Craigwell House. The path crosses a drive to go half left, then right, then half left again to emerge onto a lane, where a signposted path slightly left then opposite leads on in the same direction through a swing gate. Follow this path between railings to cross another drive and take up the path again opposite, which descends within another 400 yards to a lane. Turn left onto this lane for a good mile downhill into Aston village, where a bridlepath leads back due north to Hambleden weir. For this path, turn left at Aston crossroads then immediately right, when you will have a mile in all back to the carpark.

8   Canal Towpath Walk

If there is one very easy long-distance walk in the Chilterns it must be the towpath to the Grand Union Canal: undemanding, different, full of interest, and impossible to lose the way.

The Grand Union enters the region at Uxbridge, on its way from Limehouse, Paddington basin, Bullsbridge and Cowley Peachey. It leaves us after 33 miles beside the tiny church at Grove, the lock before Leighton Buzzard, having travelled by Widewater, Black Jack's, Cow Roast and 'Maffers', passing junctions with the Wendover and Aylesbury arms and the nature reserves at Wilstone and Startopsend along the way. The very names intrigue as does the canal language, speaking of butties and boreholes, side pounds, winding eyes, turnover bridges, 'roses and castles' and other mysteries that hint at a life and culture alien to the modern world; and alien you will indeed find it as you drift through a world little changed since the great workhorses with their shaggy fetlocks first walked these towpaths, pulling the long strings of barges behind them. I have long determined that when I am too old and stiff to walk on the hills anymore I shall take an extended trip along the towpaths of England's canal system, walking out of the Chilterns towards Braunston and Bingley Five Rise, through the tunnels and wooded cuttings of the Midlands with their split bridges and barrel-roofed lock cottages, putting up for the night at Tam'o'the'Wood or the Durham Ox at Shrewley, and perhaps getting as far as the Shroppie and the fabled aqueduct at Pontcysyllte. (I discovered, after years of wondering, that you pronounce it 'Pontysillity'.) Once the canal gets to you it draws you back, like Wastwater, time and time again.

Good walkers might tackle the whole stretch through the Chilterns in two days, though that would leave little time for exploring. A week would be ideal, and a two-day weekend with part of the way, say the stretch from Uxbridge to Coppermill or Rickmansworth, covered on the Friday evening, would be comfortable.

Walk 25

Uxbridge station – Uxbridge lock – Denham lock – Harefield Moor – Coppermill lock – Batchworth lock – Rickmansworth – Cassiobridge Marine – Cassiobury Park – Hunton Bridge – Abbot's Langley – King's Langley – Hemel Hempstead – Berkhamsted – Northchurch – Dudswell lock – Cowroast – Tring – Bulbourne – Startopsend reserve – Marsworth – Pitstone – Ivinghoe – Cheddington – Grove – Leighton Buzzard

(32 miles approx.)

ALTERNATIVES
Diversions to Cowley, Denham village and/or Piccotts End
Return to Chorleywood station from Coppermill
End at Rickmansworth station
End at Tring station

Uxbridge lock no. 88 is within five minutes' walk of Uxbridge Metropolitan station. Turn right on leaving the station, and the old High Street will bring you down to the canal at the bridge beside a pub called the Treaty House. There are twelve locks and eighteen bridges between Uxbridge and the pretty stretch where the canal runs through Cassiobury Park at Watford, where Watford Metropolitan is some ten minutes away. (Both Uxbridge and Watford Metropolitan stations return you to the terminus at Baker Street, as does Rickmansworth station which you will pass along the way. Further on at King's Langley, Apsley, Berkhamsted and Tring the line returns you to Euston.) You will find that every bridge has its number on an oval plate on the bridge arch, and at each lock there is a number as well as a name. Our route proceeds back towards lock no. 1 at Braunston, where the Grand Union starts.

Uxbridge lock makes an attractive start to our journey, with its tidy permanent moorings, lock cottage and turnover bridge. There is always a good gathering of brightly painted narrowboats to be seen here. *The way lies north, but if you are sufficiently interested you might choose, now or on another occasion, to walk the 3 miles south from here to Cowley Peachey Junction where the Slough arm goes off to the west. Cowley lock no. 89 is the end of a 27 mile level stretch from London; here the canal begins its ascent out of the Colne valley and over the Chilterns, an ascent so gradual as to be imperceptible, which culminates at the Tring summit. There is an inn at Cowley called the Paddington Packet Boat, commemorating the packet boat service that once ran daily from Cowley to London. Drawn by teams of four great horses the boats were both reliable and, for the time, swift, and if a trifle damp at times they were at least more comfortable than the stage coaches which were then the alternative. Both were put out of business, of course, by the railways.*

Hardly a step into the Chilterns from Uxbridge is Denham lock, deepest on the canal at 11 feet 1 inch. Denham is surrounded by water: Frays river, the infant River Misbourne, the River Colne, and several worked-out gravel pits left flooded after years of digging. There were two mills at Denham when the *Domesday Book* was written, and several features have survived from subsequent centuries which make Denham village worth a visit if you would consider a detour so early in the walk.

A clear footpath leaves the towpath some 200 yards beyond the turnover bridge no. 182; it follows the Misbourne for 500 yards, crosses a lane and goes through Court Farm to come out in the village, where you will find the first pubs and snacks of the day. The 'turnover' bridges, incidentally, were built to take the towpath from one bank to the other. The draft horses would have plodded over these narrow bridges still pulling their boats, and you can trace the rubbing of the heavy tow ropes in the soft bricks of the bridge coping.

Denham church has a Norman tower and thirteenth-century font and an unusual Doom painting, rather the worse for wear, of the sea giving up her dead. There is also a brass to Dame Agnes Jordan, last Abbess of Syon, one of the only two known brasses to an abbess in England. In the churchyard is the mass grave of seven members of the Marshall family, farmers, all hacked to death by a mad travelling man one bright May morning in 1870 because the father had stopped the cost of a broken tool from his wages. Nikolaus Pevsner calls Denham one of the most attractive villages near London in any direction, and who can argue with him? If you find the village vaguely familiar, with its old pubs around the village green, timber-framed cottages and humpbacked bridge over the little stream, stop and ask yourself what films you've been watching lately. Between the wars and in the Forties and Fifties Denham was the centre of the British film industry. Alexander Korda had a house nearby, and built the Denham Studios, now the home of Rank Zerox, a mile or two away towards Rickmansworth on the A412. With Pinewood Studios only 3 miles away towards Slough, the sight of cameras rolling has been all too familiar in this village.

Betweem Denham deep lock and Stockers, no. 82, the canal traverses Harefield Moor, a reedy wasteland of much interest to naturalists. Birds over-winter on the worked-out gravel pits that lie to either side of the waterway, and though the stretches of water are largely hidden by reeds and by the trees and hedges that edge the towpath, one can hear the skeins of geese come honking in and sometimes the whistle and beat of swans' wings over the water. There are plenty of pubs along this stretch: the Horse and Barge by bridge no. 180 at Widewater lock, the Fisheries at Coppermill lock no. 84, and the Whip and Collar just along the road to the north-west of Springwell lock no. 83. At Black Jack's, lock no. 85, there are some of the most sought-after moorings on the canal, which is no surprise when you see the pretty thatched cottages and the old mill, now a restaurant specializing in Italian cuisine and serving vegetables from the mill garden. Customers at Black Jack's are privileged to wander with their drinks about the gardens and across the tiny bridges of a most delightful water garden landscaped and maintained by the proprietor, and at night a miniature waterwheel splashes and tinkles in the coloured lights around the restaurant, scattering droplets into the stream.

At Coppermill lock the weir and millshoot once powered a paper mill, but with the advent of the canal the mill turned instead to beating out copper sheets for sheathing boat hulls, hence the name Coppermill. Beyond the lock the towpath is bordered by cottage gardens bright with flowers, and even the gaunt factories coming right down to the opposite bank are softened by the lapping water and the trees and patches of waterweed that seem to spring from their very walls. You have about 3 miles to walk from Coppermill to Batchworth lock no. 81 and the nearby Rickmansworth station, which could well mark the end of this stage of the walk. Personally I would follow the canal, *but walkers who*

*have had enough of the towpath can escape at Coppermill and make
their way across country to Chorleywood Metropolitan station,
about 4 miles away.*

*To do this, leave the towpath at the Fisheries Inn and take the FP
signposted across the carpark. Cross the factory service road at a
stile, and you will see ahead at a gap in the hedge the notice board of a
private angling club. A path here goes due west on a narrow isthmus,
at places no more than 6 feet wide, between two great lakes. These are
fishermen's lakes, where enthusiasts sit out all night in the season with
thermos flasks and sleeping bags waiting for the dawn. (See also Walk
no. 15.)*

*After a lonely mile the path emerges onto the Old Uxbridge Road,
reduced to a pleasant backwater by the A412, which has been
superseded in its turn by the M25. Turn right here for about 800 yards
until you come to the broad verge of the A412. Take advantage of the
traffic lights at Maple Cross to get over this busy road, and continue to
the foot of a pedestrian bridge where a private road and bridlepath go
off left to Woodoaks Farm. Make up here towards the old farm
buildings ahead, bearing right past the farmhouse to the last opening
in the old brick wall, which gives onto the bridleway. Turn right again
here to make up between fields to where trees crown the ridge ahead,
then right again through these trees until you can turn left onto the
long footbridge that carries the footpath high over the M25.*

*At the far side of the bridge, ignore the paved path and instead
cross the stile, which gives onto meadowland. Keeping always ahead
(north-west), this path crosses three fields separated by fences, and
when after a mile houses appear in plain view ahead the path goes
right over a stile and up a narrow track into The Swillett, by the Stag
inn. Turn left through the village (note the air raid siren high on a pole
beside The Swillett Stores; they had evacuees here during the war),
and follow round until Heronsgate Road becomes Shire Lane and a
signpost announces 'Chorleywood Station ½m'.*

*For interest and variety this 10 mile walk between Uxbridge and
Chorleywood stations takes a lot of beating. Waterside inns, locks
and narrowboats, followed by the rural scene of cornfields, haybarns
and creeper-clad farmhouse, even the bridge over the motorway and
the suburban metroland of The Swillett and Chorleywood – all make
for a memorable outing. However, this is supposed to be a canalside
walk, and for those following the canal the best is yet to come.*

Onwards from Coppermill the waterway traverses a reedy

wasteland towards the outskirts of Rickmansworth. In season there are vast stretches of orange balsam in the hinterland, tall spikes of codlins and cream and Queen Anne's lace beside the towpath; swifts skim to and fro across the water and where, on the quiet bank opposite, trees droop to the canal's surface, their branches and roots give shelter to ducks, grebes, coots and moorhen. It was here along the towpath between Stockers lock and Batchworth, where the canal skirts Rickmansworth Aquadrome, that I first saw deadly nightshade, a striking and malevolent plant quite different from its effete, red-berried 'Woody' cousin.

You meet few people here, especially on weekdays, but you will be unfortunate if, at some stage, you fail to see a narrowboat 'locking through'. Indeed, since this operation can easily take half an hour when conducted by amateurs, and the speed limit on the canal is 4mph, you may pass and be passed by the same boats several times in the course of the day. I have made some good friends this way.

Batchworth, one of the prettier locks, is almost in the heart of Rickmansworth. Here the rivers Colne and Chess make a confluence with the Gade, which will keep company with us now, though not always obviously, to Hemel Hempstead. There is a small side lock into the Chess, and several weirs, and smooth garden lawns come down to the waters' edge. After a dull stretch from lock 79, Common Moor, where the canal is edged by warehouses and back-garden fences, it bursts into life again at Cassiobridge Marina which heralds the entry to Cassiobury Park. The house at Cassiobury, formerly the home of the Earls of Essex, was demolished sixty years ago when the Park was acquired by Watford for use as a public open space. Very lovely it is, too, with its broad greensward, avenue of limes, and river and canal winding through.

The two waterways continue past Grove Mill, where the gaunt old millhouse has been converted into chic waterside apartments, to Lady Capel's Bridge, which marks the end of Cassiobury Park. This ornate bridge was one of the concessions demanded by the then Earl (family name Capel) for allowing the passage of the Grand Union over his land. It is surely the most ornamental canal bridge in England, with shapely stone balustrading and parapet, and lovely sweeping arch.

From here the canal emerges into open country, ducks under the M25 and runs in quick succession through Hunton Bridge, Abbot's Langley and King's Langley, a stretch where there are numerous pubs, including the Little Red Lion close by bridge 155, and two interesting churches. Abbot's Langley church of St Lawrence, west of Hunton Bridge lock 72, has twelfth-century nave arcades, an octagonal perpendicular font and fourteenth-century wallpaintings; while at All Saints, King's Langley, there is a magnificent Jacobean pulpit and the tomb chest of Edmund de Langley, brother of the Black Prince, decorated with thirteen alabaster shields. There is also a railway station at King's Langley, adjacent to lock 70/bridge 159, on the Euston line.

As the scenery deteriorates rather beyond King's Langley and you will by now have walked some 15 miles, without diversions, from Uxbridge, you might like to end your journey here and leave the rest for another day. Unless you mean to walk the whole length of the towpath, you could do worse than to skip the stretch from King's Langley to Hemel and recommence at Berkhamsted, where again the canal is only yards from the railway station, but if you are taking in the whole and your trip is leisurely you might consider a diversion from Two Waters to Piccotts End, 2½ miles away. You would see something of both the new and the old towns at Hemel Hempstead, and at the end of your walk at Piccotts End, there is an Elizabethan painted room in what is believed to have been a pilgrims' hospice. *For this diversion you should leave the towpath at bridge 151 and simply follow the River Gade north through the town as closely as you can. It will take you through Gadebridge Park to Piccotts End. To see the old town, divert right along the road from the roundabout at the beginning of Gadebridge Park, turning left at the first opportunity. The first available left turn, when you have seen all you want, will return you to the park and the river, or the road through the old town will also bring you to Piccotts End. St Mary's church in old Hemel Hempstead is said to be one of the finest Norman churches in Hertfordshire. This old town is also a sad reminder of what Hemel Hempstead was before the new town was created after the war. But we all need somewhere to live.*

Back on the towpath at Winkwell bridge 147 beyond Boxmoor Top lock, there is a wheel-operated swing bridge, worth a look, and also the Three Horseshoes inn. The River Bulbourne now keeps pace with the canal to Berkhamsted, 4 miles on from Hemel, where canal and river flow together under the ramparts of Berkhamsted Castle. This historic site is no more, today, than a green mound encircled by a ditch and decorated with a few remaining lumps of stone and flint. But the site is historic because it was here that William the Conqueror, on his way to London from Hastings, was crowned King of England in 1066. Berkhamsted was given to William's cousin, Geoffrey of Mortain, who had the castle built here. Thomas à Becket had it pulled down and a sturdier one built, which in its time housed numerous kings and queens and had Geoffrey Chaucer for Clerk of Works. The castle fell into disuse as a royal residence in the sixteenth century in favour of the more comfortable Ashridge, stolen at the Dissolution from the Bonhommes, and was finally ruined by Cromwell's cannon in the Civil War.

Since Boxmoor the canal has been climbing steadily towards the Tring summit level where it crosses the Chiltern hills. Every boat that goes over the summit moves an unbelievable 200,000 gallons of water through the locks, and the replacement of this water in the comparatively dry Chilterns was a challenge to the canal builders. Their remedy was to sink a borehole at Northchurch to the south of the hills and make reservoirs of the marl lakes at Marsworth, Wilstone and Startopsend to the north, tapped via Tringford pumping station. (More detail about this is given in Walk no. 4.)

Dudswell lock, beyond Northchurch, is the start of the Tring Development Scheme initiated by the British Waterways Board as a shop window for the waterways and to encourage the development of a canal leisure industry. The towpath was smartened up and tidied and a new marina dug at the next lock, no. 46 Cowroast, introducing an altogether out-of-place air of efficiency to what has until now been a delightful dream world. Contrast the smartness of Cowroast with the easy, go-as-you-please atmosphere of the marina at Cassiobridge and you will see what I mean.

However, the old Toll Office still stands at Cowroast, a name, incidentally, which W. Branch Johnson in his *Hertfordshire* of 1970 describes as a corruption of 'Cow Rest', a drovers' rest with cattle pens on the way from the Midlands to Smithfield. This is borne out by the swinging signboard at the nearby Cow Roast inn which plainly says 'The Cow Roast'. A Buckinghamshire man, John Westcar of Whitchurch, who raised prize cattle at Creslow Great Pasture north of Aylesbury, was the first farmer to use the new canal to transport his animals to market to save them going on the hoof, thus preventing the loss of condition brought about by the 50 mile trek to London. One of Farmer Westcar's prize oxen fetched the great sum of £100 at Smithfield in 1799.

Soon after Cowroast the waterway enters the Tring cutting, a stretch of silence in green shade with kingfishers, bright hedgerows and the occasional fisherman. After a long mile the canal is crossed at bridge 135 by the road leading to Tring station, 500 yards to the north-east but going on 2 miles from the centre of Tring, which lies in the other direction. If you have walked from King's Langley this could be the end of your journey for today, but still to come is the flight of locks taking the canal abruptly down the escarpment, which is so much steeper than the gentle dip slope up from Hemel; also to come are the great reservoirs at Wilstone, and Bulbourne and Marsworth junctions where the Wendover and Aylesbury arms strike off to the west.

The Wendover arm was constructed as a feeder for the main canal, though it came to be used extensively for the carriage of goods, and at one time there were warehouses and a thriving wharf at the Wendover terminal. Unfortunately it was built on a poorly puddled bottom over chalk, which leaked badly after a few years, and far from topping up the main arm (there was a good spring, still flowing, at the Wendover terminal) it was a constant drain. In 1904 the section beyond Tringford pumping station was stopped off and allowed to go dry, so the arm is navigable for small boats only and that for not much more than a mile from the junction at Bulbourne. However, it is still possible to walk the course of the Wendover arm from Wendover to Bulbourne, as described in Walk no. 7.

By contrast, the Aylesbury arm, which leaves the canal at Marsworth junction another mile along the way, is navigable all the way to Aylesbury boat basin. This is a 'narrow' canal, built to the 7 foot standard. That is not to say the canal itself is only 7 foot wide throughout its length, but that the locks are 7 foot wide, as they are on what remains of the Wendover arm. By the early 1950s the Aylesbury arm was in a sorry state. The Aylesbury Boat Company and Willow Wren Carrying Company put pressure on the British Transport Commission, then responsible for the canal system, to repair the locks and dredge the bottom, and as a result commercial carrying was resumed for a short time. Latterly the Aylesbury Canal Society members, who lease the boat basin from the BWB, have been active in preserving the arm, and today the whole 6 mile stretch from 'Maffers' to Aylesbury is navigable and the towpath in good repair. The walk from Tring to Aylesbury, with a convenient railway station at either end, is one of the best I know for 'Knitting up the ravelled sleave of care'. Taken once a year with a packet of sandwiches and a thermos of something hot it makes unrivalled medicine for the work-worn psyche.

Originally all Britain's canals were constructed to this 7 foot standard, with the canal narrowboats built to suit. The canal system owes its existence to James Brindley, a north-country millwright who learned his craft under the Duke of Bridgewater when building a canal to the Duke's instructions to carry coal to Manchester from his mines at Worsley. Brindley's canals were entirely artificial; he refused to make use of rivers or any natural water, except to top up his precious channels, going to excessive lengths to build tunnels and aqueducts to avoid union with any river he came across. 'Natural' water was unreliable, he said, being apt to flood or run dry according to season. A near illiterate genius, he did all his calculations in his head and his drawings on what served in his day for the backs of envelopes. When faced with a difficulty he would retire to bed and there he would remain, sometimes for days, until his problem was solved. In this manner over 300 miles of working canals were built to his direction, together with such tunnels, bridges, locks, cuttings, embankments or boat lifts as were necessary. But Brindley had nothing to do with the Grand Union Canal, which started life as the Grand Junction in the 1790s, twenty years after Brindley's death, and was built under the supervision of William Jessop.

This Grand Junction, built to join the canal systems of the Midlands and the north with those of Oxford and London, was conceived as a wide canal with locks to a 14 foot standard, enabling a double row of boats to pass together ('breasted up' was the term); but it was never the success hoped of, having only a few years of unrivalled prosperity before losing its most profitable business to the new railways. By the mid 1800s the writing was on the wall for the whole system.

Even without the diversion of the two side arms, the route northwards from the Grand Junction Arms at Bulbourne by bridge 133 is full of interest. For much of the way the towpath borders Marsworth reservoir, one of the group of marl lakes that make up Startopsend nature reserve. The chief attraction of marl lakes, which are found only on chalk and limestone, is their beautifully clear water. Fish, insects and water plants flourish in such friendly habitat, and these in turn give food to large populations of wintering and breeding birds.

Startopsend is a National Nature Reserve under the care of the Nature Conservancy Council and leased by them from the BWB. The nature trail is just under 2 miles long and takes in part of the towpath (see Walk no. 4).

The NCC leaflet tells us that up to 15,000 gulls roost on Wilstone reservoir, and overall they can expect up to 1000 ducks, including mallard, teal, shoveller, tufted, pochard, wigeon, and some goosander. In spring you can expect redshank, greenshank, dunlin, ruff and sandpiper; the little ringed plover has nested since 1938, osprey and marsh harrier have been seen, and there are colonies of great crested grebe. Add to this a heronry, and plant communities of yellow flag, water figwort, pink floating bistort and orange balsam, and rarer marsh flora (including early marsh orchids), and several species of rushes and sedges, and you will begin to understand the importance of these wetlands.

Past the reservoirs, where the White Lion stands on bridge 132 at Startopsend, you should cross over to the east bank towpath unless you intend to divert along the Aylesbury arm. The quieter Red Lion can be found in the pretty canalside village of Marsworth, just off the towpath at bridge 130. Also at Marsworth, across the bridge on the west bank, is a canalside shop and café of a type once common along the Cut but now very rare indeed. (See Walk no. 4 again for a route taking in this area.)

Northwards now the canal falls steadily through another seven locks to pass well and truly out of the Chilterns at Church lock 29 at Grove. On the way it passes Pitstone and the tall slim chimneys of Castle Cement, Ivinghoe and Cheddington, which in 1962 was the site of the Great Train Robbery – none of them close enough to visit. The most interesting sight, once the tower of Ivinghoe church is past, is probably the Whipsnade lion cut into the chalk hillside away to the east, marking the site of the wild life park.

Mentmore Towers, to the west, can be reached by footpath from Horton lock 31, a walk of 1½ miles each way; make sure you are choosing a day when the mansion is open to the public. Also accessible from Horton lock is Cheddington station, being a mile or so to the south-west.

The church at Grove, listed as a fourteenth-century chapel with a later bell turret, was made redundant in 1971; its bell was taken to Westonbirt, Glos. and its Norman font to Llantrisant. This church, St Michael's, was the smallest church in Buckinghamshire. It is now occupied as a private residence.

We are now well and truly out of the Chilterns, the hills left far behind, 14½ miles from Berkhamsted. The best choice now is to carry on a further 1½ miles to bridge 114 at Leighton Linslade where you will find Leighton Buzzard station 300 yards or so to the west, for return, as from Cheddington, to Euston.

The Nicholson/Ordnance Survey *Guide to the Waterways*, issued in three volumes, gives a detailed description of Britain's entire canal system.

9   A Chilterns Hundred

This 100 mile circular tour was pioneered in the late Eighties by
Mr Jimmy Parsons of Amersham, a man with many years of
walking in the Chilterns behind him and an intimate knowledge of
the terrain.

In his book, *A Chilterns Hundred*, published with the financial
backing of the Chiltern Society and the Thames & Chilterns
Tourist Board, Mr Parsons takes us, with the help of half inch
sketch maps, on a circular tour in seven stages in distances varying
between 11 and 18 miles. He juggles the footpaths to keep us
almost entirely from road walking, choosing where possible the
quieter and lesser-known ways. Yet we see the best of the Chiltern
scenery, and where the route keeps to the lower slopes to encircle
the hills rather than striding the ridge, it does so to lead us by
kindlier paths. Indeed, some of the upper routes are so walked out
in places that there is little pleasure in them for the greater part of
the year. Only under frost does the view compensate for the mud
along parts of the Ridgeway, for example, where trail riders and
other mudlarkers make life unpleasant for the walker.

You will recognize in the following brief description sections of
the Icknield Way, the Oxfordshire Way, and other walks outlined
here in *Walking in the Chilterns*, but don't make the mistake of
thinking that you can look out a couple of maps and piece together
Mr Parsons' route from the brief details given here; he has
obviously brought much time and trouble to the working out of his
tour, and the few extra pennies spent on his book will pay
tremendous dividends in enjoyment.

From a suggested beginning at Amersham Metropolitan station,
the route makes a fine start through the Chiltern Forest and along
the Chess Valley to the picture villages of Latimer and Chenies,
skirts Chorleywood towards the Chilterns Open Air Museum at

Newland Park, and goes on through Chalfont St Giles to finish the section at Jordans, near the Quaker Guest House and the Youth Hostel.

The second stage takes us on via Hedgerley, Burnham Beeches, Littleworth Common and Hedsor to cross the Thames at Cookham Bridge and follow the river bank along what is arguably the best stretch of the Thames, until the towpath crosses to the other bank again at Spade Oak. There being no ferryman now to pole us across, the route keeps to the south bank to go on up Winter Hill and through Quarry Wood to Marlow. Those with any knowledge of the area will recognize that by any standard this must be a marvellous day's walk.

Stage three goes from Marlow to Stonor, first along the river bank then by woodland and field paths to Medmenham and Hambleden, and on to the quiet, remote villages of Skirmett, with its white-daubed cottages, Turville with its windmill, and Fingest with its twin saddleback tower to the church – lovely villages all, little touched by time, and hidden away along wooded lanes where you might as easily meet a fox or a pheasant as another human soul.

Stonor to Watlington, the fourth stage, goes on through equally remote country to Maidensgrove, the Warburg Nature Reserve, Nettlebed and Nuffield, before striking north to pass under the walls of the gaunt old fifteenth-century grammar school (now a primary school) at Ewelme, where it is impossible not to stop to investigate the church and almshouses, before following the Icknield Way on to Watlington.

The Pyrton Driftway takes us from Watlington at the start of stage 5, on the way to Christmas Common, Ibstone Common and Stokenchurch before we take to the quiet country around Bennett End and Radnage where the great golden ball above West Wycombe church and the Dashwood Mausoleum dominate all. Then we find the Icknield Way once more, to come gloriously to the Lions of Bledlow and on to finish the stage at Princes Risborough.

Stage six could simply follow the ridge from Princes Risborough to Wendover and Tring, but instead we are taken more adventurously by Lacey Green and the Hampdens and through the woods to Wendover, before following the Wendover arm of the Grand Union Canal to Tring, with the chance of a glance at the Rothschild village of Halton along the way.

The last stage, the long walk from Tring back to Amersham,

winds through Wigginton and Cholesbury and glimpses the lovely old moated farmhouse at Dundridge Manor, before going on by field and woodland to Swan Bottom, The Lee and Great Missenden. And yet we are not done, for there is still the thrill of Little Missenden, Shardeloes and Old Amersham before this very satisfying journey is at last over.

Take my advice and try this walk soon; this is going to be very popular, and those of us who have seen the mire of the Lyke Wake or the Pennine Way over Penyghent, not to mention our own poor Ridgeway, will appreciate the advisability of getting in on this one early. Taken as a whole, it would make a fine seven-day spring or autumn break, though it will readily be recognized that the route is so organized that the individual stages could be walked singly over a period, as an ongoing project.

10   BBONT and the Chiltern Society

More than most people, walkers are dependent upon local conservation and amenity societies, so it is fitting that this last chapter should concern itself with the Chiltern Society and the County Naturalists' Trusts, whose members were defending their own patch long before the Green Revolution was heard of. The Herts & Middx Naturalists' Trust is active in the south-east corner of the Chilterns, but the Trust best known throughout the region is BBONT (BeeBont, as it is fondly referred to), the Berks, Bucks & Oxfordshire Naturalists' Trust.

A walker would be dull of soul indeed to lack some interest in the countryside; architecture, birds, butterflies, deep woodland, the vast sweep of hills and heathlands, all enchant and enthrall. But those who walk the year round in all weathers and seasons most often mark the months by the wild flowers, and for such as these a visit to the BBONT reserves is a must. Chiltern beech woods and chalk downlands are particularly rich in flora; there are sixteen species of orchids to be found, including the monkey orchid, military orchid (two of its only three British sites are watched over by BBONT) and the saprophytic ghost orchid, also coral root and red helleborine. Pasque flower is there, and the Chiltern gentian, and somewhere along the Thames watermeadows chequered fritillaries and the loddon lily grow. All this is in addition to the more common flowers of heath, field and woodland.

In the BBONT Reserves Handbook I have counted seventeen Reserves and SSSI's within the area of the Chilterns listed as Open to Members Only, including a lake with a hide overlooking upwards of 1,000 duck of various species; a pond with smooth newts; an ancient forest with fallow deer and muntjac, wood white and black hairstreak butterflies, and most woodland warblers including the nightjar; an area of neutral grassland with a remarkable population of green veined orchids; a coppiced beech wood with badger setts; an adjacent pair of ancient meadows, one with a fen community of early marsh orchids, meadowsweet and a variety of rushes, and the other with quaking grass, pepper saxifrage and several wild orchids; a south-facing chalk slope of very uncharacteristic beech wood with over 200 species of plants recorded including a remarkable display of yellow birdsnest orchid; a meadow with adders tongue fern; an old chalk pit with many orchids, knapweed broomrape and Chiltern gentian; and a combination of woodland, rough grassland and fen where flue dust dumped over a long period from a nearby works has made a potash-rich habitat where a total of 150 plant species has been recorded, together with 69 species of birds, over 30 moths, 20 butterfly species, 5 dragonfly and damselfly, 4 amphibians and 14 different mammals. All you need to do to be made free of these and the other closed reserves is to become a member of BBONT (address on p.127).

However, apart from the closed reserves there are many in the care of BBONT that are open to the public, and I am able to give the locations of those reserves here. When visiting them please remember these rules, which are also printed in the Reserves Handbook:

1. Visitors must comply with any reasonable request of a warden or other representative of BBONT.

2. Visitors may not pick, collect, take away or introduce any plant or animal onto Trust Reserves without written authority from the Conservation Officer. Frequently Trust reserves are used for research, and any unauthorized activities could seriously damage the results.

3. Visitors should take care to avoid disturbing birds or other animals, especially when they are breeding, and search should not be made for nests. Hides may not be erected.

4. Visitors should avoid damage to vegetation by keeping to paths wherever provided; close all gates, and avoid trespass or disturbance to adjacent property.

5. Dogs may be prohibited in the Reserve, and this is stated in the individual reserve description. If this is not the case, dogs are permitted provided they are on a lead.

6.   Guard against fire risks. Plantations, woodlands and heaths are highly inflammable; every year areas burn because of casually dropped cigarettes, matches or pipe ash. Special care is necessary at times of high fire risk when special precautions may be in force on some reserves.

7.   Leave no litter. All litter is unsightly, and some is dangerous.

8.   BBONT accepts no responsibility for any loss, injury or damage, howsoever caused, which may be sustained while visiting the Reserves.

The following, then, are the BBONT Reserves within the area of the Chilterns open to the public, starting with the South Oxfordshire Region.

Warburg Reserve
Nr. Bix, OS sheet 175, GR 720880. This is the largest reserve and one with a full-time warden. There are 247 acres of grassland and mixed deciduous woodland clothing both slopes of a dry valley. The mixed deciduous woodland includes oak, ash, beech, birch, field maple and yew, with understorey of hazel, dogwood, wayfaring tree, spindle, hawthorn, buckthorn and wild privet. There are 15 species of orchid as well as Chiltern gentian, and the reserve is rich in birds, butterflies, badgers, foxes, muntjac, adders, grass snakes and slow worms.

Hartslock
Nr. Goring on Thames, OS sheet 175, GR 607786. Dogs should be kept on a lead while sheep are grazing, and visitors must not cross the temporary fencelines where research work is undertaken. This is rich chalk grassland on south and south-west facing slopes, with views of the Thames Valley and Goring Gap. Over twenty species of butterfly are recorded, including chalkhill blue and adonis; plant species include cowslip, autumn gentian, harebell, clustered bellflower, birdsfoot trefoil, dodder, and bastard toadflax.

Chinnor Hill
65.5 acres bought by the Trust in 1965 and scheduled as an SSSI in 1972. OS sheet 165, GR 766005. Now mainly scrub with an area of grassland on the hilltop, this was once neutral or acid grassland on

clay with flints at the top and chalk downland with juniper on the scarp face. Where the scrub is not too dense, chalk grassland plants such as rock rose, thyme, carline thistle, autumn gentian, Chilterns gentian and bee and frog orchids still survive. Also there are seven species of warblers recorded, buntings, thrushes, and all the usual woodland species. Two Saxon burial mounds are on the summit.

Boarstall Decoy

This is in the Aylesbury Vale Region, north-east of Oxford, on lease from the National Trust. A charge is made for non-members of either BBONT or the NT. OS sheet 164, GR 623151. Here is one of only four working duck decoys in the country, now used to capture duck for ringing and release. The surrounding woodland is rich in birdlife and mammals. The path can, with assistance, be used by visitors in wheelchairs.

Bernwood Meadows

Approx. 4 miles south of Boarstall, OS sheet 164, GR 606110. Visitors should keep to the two public footpaths from mid-May until the hay has been harvested. Dogs are not allowed when stock is grazing. Two neutral meadows are bordered by some ancient hedges, with a pond in each meadow. Over 100 plant species have been recorded, including twenty-three grasses, adders tongue fern and green veined orchid. Fallow deer and muntjac use the reserve, and rutting stands are clearly visible in autumn.

Oakley Parish Hedge

OS sheet 164, GR 615122. The hedge begins at the northern corner of Oakley Wood and borders the road for roughly half a mile on the south-east side. Seventeen woody species have been found in this ancient hedge, which is cared for by BBONT by agreement with the owners.

Rushbeds Wood

Near Wotton Underwood, ENE of Boarstall, OS sheet 164, GR 668157. Here 114 acres of ancient woodland are open to the public along the rides, with 197 species of plants recorded excluding mosses, lichens and fungi. It is very good for butterflies, including black hairstreak. There are some fallow deer, and populations of both fox and muntjac.

Chequers

The Chilterns Region includes this site, south-west of Wendover, OS sheet 165, GR 830055, where 83 acres of grassland and box coombes are managed by BBONT by agreement with the Trustees of the Chequers Estate. There is a public FP running from the point of entry round the head of the coombe, across the western drive to Chequers and on to Ellesborough. The grassland areas above the coombe are open to BBONT members; a permit is required to enter the box areas. Chalk grassland plants include squinancywort, rock rose, thyme, vipers bugloss, deadly nightshade and musk orchid, and the box areas contain a rich assemblage of chalk-loving bryophytes. This box community is thought to be one of only three truly native British sites.

Grangelands & Pulpit Hill

These adjoin the Chequers reserve. Grangelands is open to the public, but the reserve on Pulpit Hill is open to BBONT members only. There is a good display of chalk-loving plants and butterflies, and this is one of the few places where juniper is successfully regenerating.

Aston Clinton Ragpits

North-east of Wendover, OS sheet 165, GR 888108. Six acres formerly worked for chalk freestoned ('rag'), now colonized by a rich assemblage of herbs, shrubs and invertebrates. Among twenty-seven butterfly species recorded are common and chalkhill blues, Duke of Burgundy fritillary, and marbled white. There are nine species of orchid, also cowslip and Chiltern gentian. This small site is close to Wendover Woods, and could be incorporated in Walk no. 8, as could:

Dancersend

OS sheet 165, GR 900095, owned by the RSNC and leased to BBONT. It is open to the public only along the bridleways, as indicated on the plan at the entrance. There are 79 acres of woodland and good chalk grassland with the rides well maintained.

Weston Turville Reservoir
OS sheet 165, GR 862096. This is managed by BBONT by agreement with the British Waterways Board, and is a scheduled SSSI. Open to the public only along the perimeter path, this Reserve is the subject of Walk no. 7.

The last two reserves are in the South Bucks Region.

Gomm Valley
South-east of High Wycombe on the A40 towards Beaconsfield, OS sheet 175, GR 898922, here are 10 acres of herb-rich chalk grassland, particularly interesting for its butterflies (over 30 species recorded) and moths (over 180 species, including bee hawk moth). Butterflies include a thriving colony of dark green fritillary, also green hairstreak, small blue, and marbled white. There are also glowworms, slow worms, and common lizards, and the site is good for birds, particularly flocks of overwintering thrushes.

Long Grove Wood
At Seer Green, OS sheet 175, GR 963917, this is a fragment of the coppiced mixed deciduous woodland which once covered the Chilterns. Much of the tree cover springs from old coppice stools. There are some bluebells and many fungi.

Members of BBONT will know that I have given only the briefest summary of the details in their Reserves Handbook, and have not touched on any of the Berkshire nor many of the Oxfordshire Reserves such as Iffley Island and Meadows or the Memorial Reserves within Oxford city limits. New to the Reserves Handbook in 1989 and deserving special mention is:

College Lake Wildlife Centre
This reserve is under the joint care of BBONT and the Castle Cement Company (Pitstone) Ltd. OS sheet 165, GR 935139. This conservation area is within easy walking distance of Tring station and is easily visited in conjunction with Walk no. 4, as it is near the Tring Reservoir. College Lake differs from the other reserves in that it has been specifically set out for public access, including wheelchair access. Utilizing over 100 acres of deep quarry workings below the Chiltern escarpment, the reserve is subsidized by Castle Cement and is under the care of their Conservation Officer, Mr Graham Atkins. With financial support from the

Company and the help of BBONT volunteers, Mr Atkins has designed and laid out a very interesting and diverse wildlife centre on this rapidly regenerating terrain.

First, the reserve is on a migratory flightpath, so deep water ditches and a 25 acre lake with islands, nesting rafts and man-made shingle beaches attract increasing numbers of nesting and wintering birds, now including redshank and little ringed plover, which can be viewed from the various hides. Second, nature trails wind through habitats of marsh, rough grassland, scrub and unregenerated quarrybank; the new grassland, much of it on steep, rough slopes, is kept tidy by rabbits and by flocks of rare breed sheep. These sheep survive better on the sparse feeding than would commercial breeds. Third, a tree stock has been built up from cuttings taken, as commercially grown trees would not thrive on the poor soil. Informal groups and areas of new woodland have been planted, partly from these cuttings, and many of the trees are now well grown. Every year more are added to the stock. Fourth, in the Visitor Centre are cases of fossils and animal bones found on site as earth was moved and trees planted, sieved out from the soil by the volunteer workers during their tea-breaks.

Lastly, there is the College Lake Arable Weed Project, the Warden's special interest and what makes this Wildlife Centre that bit different. In a working museum of farming, five third-of-an-acre plots have been planted with roots and traditional long strawed cereals and are farmed in rotation using the old hand tools and horse-drawn implements of which Mr Atkins has a very creditable collection on show. Before the Second World War cornfields were bright with annual weeds which are seldom seen today. Field cornflower, corncockle, pheasants eye, corn buttercup, shepherd's needle, corn marigold: 'scarce and decreasing' is what Collins Pocket Guide has to say of these, giving them two stars for rarity. Organic farming of the long strawed cereals, in which they flourished, should encourage these and the better known wild flowers such as pimpernel, camomile and field poppies to establish themselves here for our future pleasure.

An Open Day is held at College Lake annually at Lammastide (nearest Saturday to August 1st), when the Centre is en fête, with the rare breed sheep shampooed and curled and enthusiasts engaged in morris dancing, rural crafts, etc. Apart from that, the Centre is open every Sunday from 10am to 5pm. Because of the

Mines & Quarries Safety Regulations it is essential that all visitors obtain a permit from the Warden's hut in the carpark before entering this reserve. To get there from Tring station, turn right from the station concourse 200 yards or so along the road to a left turn signposted 'Pitstone'. A mile and a half along this road brings you to a T-junction where you turn left again for another 500 yards, when you will find the entrance to the Wildlife Centre on the right – a green-painted iron gate just past the railway bridge. Drivers should take the B488 north-east from the roundabout on the A41 on the Aylesbury side of Tring, where the entrance is found on the left just past the canal bridge and Junction Arms at Bulbourne. Do visit the Centre; where else would you see a restored, genuine, wheeled shepherd's hut?

Long before BBONT became involved with this site, however, members of the Chiltern Society were cooperating with Castle Cement to regenerate the worked-out quarry areas here. During the late Seventies and early Eighties eighty-one experimental plots were laid out under the direction of a Chiltern Society member on the worked out floor of Quarry no 1. Several varieties of grasses and legumes were sown there to determine the quickest growing and most durable cover for the unsightly areas of underchalk, and in the light of these experiments Castle Cement subsequently had the floor of Quarry no. 2 planted with sanfoin and Quarry no. 3 with selected grasses and clovers. Much of this area is now farmed, but in a world of milk quotas, wheat surpluses and butter mountains the College Lake Wildlife Centre seems a better use for the land.

It is impossible to estimate the impact of the Chiltern Society upon the Chilterns. Founded in 1965 with the modest aim of 'Stimulating public interest in and care for the beauty, history and character of the area of the Chiltern Hills', the Society's influence can now be felt in every aspect of Chiltern life, and no walker on the hills or in Chiltern woodlands should fail to acknowledge this and give thanks.

Apart from vetting every planning application submitted to County or Parish Councils, members keep a watching brief on commons, roads and transport facilities, conservation, historic works and buildings, and water resources. The Rights of Way Group waymarks, clears, builds stiles, keeps open over 2,000 miles of footpaths and publishes (through Shire Publications) nineteen footpath maps; and the Trees and Woodlands Group in their Small Woodlands Project have, over the last five years, worked in eighty-nine Chiltern woods planting 22,000 trees and shrubs on sixty sites and thinning and coppicing on others. Mention has been made elsewhere in this book of the Chilterns Open Air Museum at Newland Park, the restoration of Lacey Green windmill, and the clearing of the River Misbourne, and you will find much other evidence of the work of Chiltern Society members on your walks in the area. Considering that money has to be raised to finance these activities and that all are dependent upon voluntary labour, the Members' achievement is remarkable.

The Chiltern Society's subscription was raised in 1989 to £8, which still seems a modest toll for inclusion in such fine company.

Bibliography

Chiltern Society Story, vol.II

Walks in Dacorum (Dacorum Borough Council, 1986)

Bryant, Sir Arthur, introduction to *Country Like This* (Friends of the Vale of Aylesbury – of which organization he was chair, 1972)

Charles, Alan, *Ridgeway Path* (Countryside Books, 1988)

Cull, Elizabeth, *Portrait of the Chilterns* (Robert Hale, 1982)

Cull, Elizabeth, *A Picture of Buckinghamshire* (Robert Hale, 1985)

Fitter, Richard, *Wild Life of the Thames Counties* (BBONT, 1985)

Gulland, Diana and Richard, *The North Buckinghamshire Way* (Bucks & West Middx branch, Ramblers' Association, 1985)

Hay, David and Joan, *Hilltop Villages of the Chilterns* (Phillimore, 1983)

Hayward, A.L., *Jordans, The Making of a Community* (Friends Home Service Committee, 1969)

Johnson, W. Branch, *Hertfordshire* (B.T. Batsford, 1970)

Massingham, H.J., *Chiltern Country* (B.T. Batsford, 1940)

Parsons, J., *A Chilterns Hundred* (Chiltern Society, 1988. Available by post from Alan Dell, 3 Swallow Lane, Stoke Mandeville, Bucks, HP22 5UW)

Perrott, D. (ed.), *Nicolsons Guide to the River Thames* (Nicolson/Ordnance Survey, 1984)

Perrott, D. (ed.), *Nicolsons Guide to the Waterways, South* (Nicolson/Ordnance Survey, 1983)

Pevsner, Nikolaus, *Buildings of England: Buckinghamshire* (Penguin, 1973)

Sharp, David, *The Thames Walk* (Ramblers' Association, 1985)

Thomas, Edward, *The Icknield Way* (Wildwood House, 1980)

Thorne, J.O., and Collocott, T.C. (ed.), *Chambers Biographical Dictionary* (Chambers, rev. edn, 1984)

Westacott, H.D., *Practical Guide to Walking the Ridgeway Path* (Footpath Publications. Available from Adstock Cottage, Adstock, nr Buckingham, MK18 2HZ)

Wotton, Vic, *To Rescue a River* (Chiltern Society, 1987)

Young, Geoffrey (ed.), *Where To Go for Wildlife in Bucks, Berks & Oxon* (BBONT, 1989)

Index